NUTS, BOLTS AND A FEW

COMMON THREADS
OF UNCOMMONLY
REMARKABLE
PEOPLE AND
SEAMLESS BRANDS

GAIR MAXWELL

PRESS
Wizard Academy Press
Austin, Texas

COPYRIGHTS

Ordering Information:
To order additional copies, contact your local bookstore, visit
www.WizardAcademyPress.com, or call 1.800.425.4769
Quantity discounts are available.

ISBN: 978-1-932226-78-2

Library of Congress Number: 2010922574

Credits:
       Cover Design: Ryan Maxwell

First printing: March 2010

CONTENTS

One Guys Opinion

When people don't like their work and love the brand they represent, it often reveals itself in front of the people who pay the bills - customers. It's an expensive way to do business since most companies spend five-to-ten times more to create a new customer as opposed to keeping an existing one.

It's not the way we do business at PropertyGuys.com.

With the help of what Gair Maxwell shares in "Nuts, Bolts And a Few Loose Screws", we have learned:

- Great brands become that way because they know great marketing begins from the inside.
- Great brands are always evolving and self-inventing, based on being in tune with emotional environments and business realities.
- Great brands are built on a profound truth.

Each and every day, our home office and franchisee network strives to honour our brand essence and leverage the combination of "nuts and bolts" thinkers with "loose screw" dreamers. That way, we have a chance to be "seamless" in everything from customer experience to web strategy and team engagement.

Commit to this approach and you will amaze yourself with the way your business gets noticed, attracts the best people and have them work together to create extraordinary results.

I sincerely hope you detect the common threads of remarkable people and seamless brands and experience the good fortune we have from applying the timeless principles of "Nuts, Bolts And a Few Loose Screws" .

Ken LeBlanc
President/CEO
PropertyGuys.com

Side One

"The blacksmith and the artist, reflect it in their art. They forge their creativity, closer to the heart. Philosophers and ploughmen, each must know his part. To sow a new mentality. closer to the heart" -**NEIL PEART**

PROLOGUE
Rattling the Humdrum

Few things are more powerful than someone who knows who they are.

Nail that down and many wonderful traits and characteristics flow from that knowledge base.

They become readily apparent.

If you know what you're all about and where you're heading, authenticity and credibility naturally result.

For one, single, solitary reason.

People trust you.

And if you have ever wondered why great leaders, companies and brands are able to emerge and endure, *trust* will always be the common denominator, seamlessly weaving its way through every key relationship.

- Relationships with customers.
- Relationships with employees.
- Relationships with partners/suppliers.
- Relationships with colleagues/communities.

Trustworthiness is but one of the many common threads shared by uncommonly successful people and brands.

Another commonality in any personal or professional success equation is the ability to operate from a spirit of possibility instead of resignation. In his acclaimed work "*Synchronicity*", best-selling author Joe Jaworski maintains true leadership "is about creating a domain in which we continually learn and become more capable of participating in our unfolding future; setting the stage for predictable miracles. According to Jaworski, this spirit is what creates synchronicity as we truly "listen" to what yearns to emerge - causing doors to fling wide open, people to connect with your ideas, creating possibilities you can vividly imagine.

Nuts, Bolts And A Few Loose Screws is an invitation to plug in, listen and trust the sound of your own voice.

It's the voice that has been whispering for years.

The voice insisting that there has got to be a better way.

To work, live and do business.

You are the kind of person who sees business as a platform capable of producing so much more than achieving quarterly sales targets. You find it increasingly difficult to stomach a mindless corporate existence governed by rigid policies and procedures that reduce or eliminate the humanity from the very people an organization claims to support and serve. Ideally, you aspire to discover a sense of purpose and meaning with the work you do and the people you do it with.

There is nothing tragically hip about the vast numbers of people who dread the thought of heading back to the shop on Monday mornings. Even before I finished high school, I believed "work" should be a place people eagerly look forward to – fully and completely. And why not? We spend so many waking hours there. But far too often, there is a sharp contrast between the wide-eyed optimism of high school students at graduation (that moment in time when all dreams are possible) and the semi-broken, disenchanted, 40-and-over corporate survivors. The ones who are ticking off days to retirement, never finding whatever it is they're looking for.

I would like to think you and I can help change that.

It begins with the imagination of business rockers who refuse to be locked up by the dream police. *Nuts, Bolts And A Few Loose Screws* is for visionaries like you who seek to serve and grow organizations with a sense of purpose, influencing the people you touch in a meaningful way. The ideas in this book are designed for business rebels who recognize the world becomes a better place when we have more companies existing for reasons beyond mere profit. When we have businesses refusing to turn cheap tricks for a quick buck and actually care about the emotional well-being of its people and the customers they serve.

Imagine cracking the source code of your company – or

any company - to actually make that happen?

Your hunt for this code becomes easier when you understand the basic premise behind the unique format of *Nuts, Bolts And A Few Loose Screws*.

"Where is it written, where is the rule that mandates a business book must be compiled in a logical, linear, sequential fashion?"

"The world of business itself hardly follows a straight line. Why not organize what appears to be a random series of essays around a central concept? Blend apparent chaos with a subtle form of order. Hey, it will be kind of like the business and branding version of Pink Floyd's "The Wall", U2's "Joshua Tree" or Green Day's "American Idiot".!

Suddenly, this literary street had a concept.

And a name.

Nuts, Bolts And A Few Loose Screws is more than loosely based on the idea of a "concept album", a format familiar to classic rock fans of the 70's and 80's. As you make your way through the book, think of it like "Tommy" or "Sgt. Pepper" where the music connects to an overall theme; the songs lyrically contributing to a single unified story.

One of the earliest concept albums was crafted in 1955 by none other than Old Blue Eyes. Frank Sinatra's "In the Wee Small Hours", consisted entirely of ballads specifically organized around a central mood of late-night isolation and aching lost love. Even the album cover strikingly reinforced that theme. The phrase "concept album" entered pop culture with a bang in 1967 when the Beatles released "Sgt. Pepper's Lonely Hearts Club Band", based more or less on an obscure radio play about the life of an ex-army bandsman. While debate continues whether "Sgt. Pepper" qualifies as a true concept album, there is no doubt the songwriting team of Lennon and McCartney inspired others to produce similar works of their own, including The Who, Styx, Nine Inch Nails, Radiohead and more.

The stories that made the final cut for Nuts, Bolts And A Few Loose Screws are designed to help you see your brand from a new perspective.

The personal or business brand you own either by accident or design.

Each essay is designed to provoke thought and invigorate your imagination about defining success in your enterprise.

Each essay is self-contained. You decide how much you want to absorb at any one time. Feel free to skip ahead, jump back and forth, or hit repeat if you want. Hey, it's your book.

This format allows you to experience the elevation of discovery without following any "how to" lists.

You already possess many of the answers to the questions that concern you most in your business and career and as such, *Nuts, Bolts And A Few Loose Screws* serves as a canvas for your imagination; a catalyst to unleash and express some far-out things you have already been thinking about but weren't sure if you were on the right track or the only one who felt that way.

Over the past decade, several unmistakable thought patterns have been detected when it comes to successful, inwardly fulfilled, entrepreneurial types. Besides the ability to inspire trust and be open to possibilities, another common thread is that true "enterprising" personalities are never satisfied being comfortably numb - existing as just another brick in the wall.

If you are a true "enterpriser", you need to make your own brand of music.

You crave it like the air you breathe.

Nuts, Bolts And A Few Loose Screws speaks to internally-motivated, life-long learners who see themselves as part of a rare breed. In your mind, possibilities come together, innovation is just a brain wave away and you have the inner will to follow through. You feel a sense of self-confidence in trusting instincts and emotions, even in the absence of explicit knowledge and information.

Your business brain often buzzes with high voltage thoughts that just need a place to land. You recognize the need to balance pragmatic, nuts and bolts business-thinking with electrifying, screwball ideas that make everyone around you exclaim, *"Whoa! ... I think you're on to something there!"* By flexing your mind muscles, you possess TNT potential to create opportunity and wealth that benefits both yourself and others. When you look at business situations, you tend to ask questions like, *"Can I make a difference?"* or *"Who will this help?"*

You evaluate an idea on more than just the money that talks.

There are abundant business and branding opportunities patiently waiting for leaders and dream weavers like you, people who are secure enough within themselves to take on the daunting challenge of building great companies and brands; ready to scale uncommon heights for the common good.

Hope this book amplifies your vision.

And rocks your world.

"As a rock star, I have two instincts, I want to have fun, and I want to change the world. I have a chance to do both." **- BONO**

1
Take a Ride on the Waterslide

Nestled amongst the pine trees just outside of Moncton, New Brunswick, Crandall University appears similar to many institutions of higher learning. Students juggle assignments and exams with part time jobs and extra curricular activities. Future lives and careers gradually take shape.

It was in this idyllic setting in the spring of 1998 that Ken LeBlanc posed an interesting question to several classmates in the business program. Ken had noticed a number of black and orange "For Sale By Owner" signs on front lawns while he was travelling to and from school. He wanted to know if it was possible to take still photographs of homes people wanted to sell – and post them on an Internet website – without using a real estate agent? He reasoned that this approach – essentially cutting out the middleman - could provide private sellers with marketing resources similar to those offered by high-priced real estate agents - but at a fraction of the cost.

Could the idea prove to be a viable business model?

Was there an opportunity to re-shape, reconfigure and change the way things were being done in the multi-billion dollar real estate industry?

Could some small town college guys with no money, industry experience or backing to speak of compete against a colossal, organized, nationwide force represented by traditional agents - while the For Sale By Owner segment was scattered piecemeal at local levels?

Essentially, Ken and his classmates were deciding whether they should gamble their future on defying Goliath?

Did they dare become David?

Your business is an extension of your beliefs.

Beliefs that form the bedrock upon which your vision is based.

As you explore *Nuts, Bolts & a Few Loose Screws* you will discover many opportunities to pause and reflect on fundamental beliefs you hold. Beliefs about what it takes to own and operate a successful business.

Regardless of your background, life experiences, where you went to school or where you came from, certain beliefs have been formed and hardened over time. It is these beliefs which ultimately guide the actions and behaviours which, in the end, determine your results in any business enterprise.

But, at this very moment, you are invited to Suspend Your Disbelief!

Suspended Disbelief is what happens each time you go to the movie theatre to enjoy one of Hollywood's latest productions. Think of the last time you went to catch a flick. You stood in line, bought the tickets. Stood in line, picked up the popcorn – entered the theatre and found a seat as far away from complete strangers as possible. You took off your coat, settled back into your chair and melted into what is known as Suspended Disbelief.

This is precisely what allowed you to enjoy the movie.

Suspended Disbelief makes it possible for you to say *"OK I can see how John Travolta and Nicholas Cage can switch their entire faces – without their wives ever finding out!"* Suspended Disbelief allows you to feel what's in the heart of Renee Zellwegger when she confesses, *"You had me at hello."*

Suspended Disbelief will never surface in a Courtroom of Logic.

The Courtroom of Logic is the box we enter whenever our brain becomes critical and judgmental of each piece of information presented to us. It's where the credibility of the people delivering that information is routinely scrutinized and second-guessed – regardless of their track record. In the Courtroom of Logic, we demand answers, data, proof, physical evidence, testimony – just the facts.

The Courtroom of Logic resides in the analytical, rational, linear, left hemisphere of our brain but when you exit that building and wander over to the other side of the street, you discover a Waterslide Park of Imagination.

Hang on.

The Waterslide Park of Imagination is where you get to splash around in the creative, chaotic, intuitive, right side of your brain. You blast your way through some plastic tubing, revelling in the chills and spills as you feel like a kid again. Vibrating with energy and enthusiasm over the dreams you envision, the Waterslide of Imagination creates a "Look Ma! No hands!" attitude as you look forward to getting a little wet and emerge soaking with enthusiasm!

"I paid my four bits to see the high divin' act...and I'm-a gonna see the high divin' act!" **-YOSEMITE SAM**

Your ability to remain in Suspended Disbelief as much as humanly possible will allow you to make the most of the time and mental energy you invest thinking about your business and your brand. Hang around the Courtroom too long and you run the risk of becoming annoyed, agitated and frustrated because the answers you hunger for don't arrive exactly when you want them.

Great brands like Apple, FedEx and Starbucks are built on a foundation of Suspended Disbelief and nurtured through the ingenuity, originality and passion of business rebels who believe in making and keeping a promise that matters. Leaders who understand at a deeper level, the core of their business model - what it stands for, and how that model becomes relevant for anyone who seeks to embrace it.

At one time, the idea of a personal computer in every home, overnight delivery and a $5.00 cup of coffee seemed anything but logical. But logic can only take any business model so far before a competitor zipping down a Waterslide of Imagination zooms right by.

A great example of this type of thinking is PropertyGuys. com, the Canadian franchising phenomenon that dared challenge the status quo of traditional real estate. Who would have believed that two university students, working part-time and with less than 100 dollars in start-up funding, could launch a real estate rebellion that would see PropertyGuys.com become

15

Canada's fastest growing franchise system, with more than 100 franchise locations in its first decade of operation? Winners of the 2008 Canadian Franchise Association "Award of Excellence", PropertyGuys.com was founded on a revolutionary promise to use the Internet to eliminate the middleman in all real estate transactions. In market after market, this radical approach is turning an entire, 90-year old industry upside down with a flat fee structure threatening the commission based MLS model.

The company founders created their own business category back in the late 1990's, recognizing the Internet could be used as a vehicle to organize a new industry called Private Sale. Despite starting out with virtually no cash, and using borrowed vans, recycled election signs and little more than an on-line bulletin board, PropertyGuys.com believed there was a better way.

All it took was a splash of Imagination.

Pushing the envelope even further, PropertyGuys.com boldly scrapped its entire brand identity built up over ten years in business, in favour of a look and feel that would capture the essence of what the company truly represents. But, it's never easy going down that waterslide without knowing for certain whether reckless abandon will be rewarded.

Would this re-brand resonate in the hearts and minds of its franchisees? If not, PropertyGuys.com was in deep trouble. Everything that had been sacrificed to that point would have been lost if the frontline failed to buy in.

The results?

Nothing short of astonishing.

The catchy, new look not only generated a massive increase in listing counts, revenues and market share, but the impact is still being felt in areas such as franchise sales, talent acquisition and national media attention. Brand momentum was also accelerated with a provocative radio campaign that challenges consumers to ask themselves why they would want to list with a "Joe Schmo" real estate agent when they could do it themselves and keep the commission in their own pockets. And this entire concept has been nourished through an ongoing training and orientation program called PropertyGuys.com University (PGU). Through a week-long, highly experiential learning process, brand essence is transferred into the hearts and minds of franchisees and their associates. At PGU, graduates learn what it means to "be the brand" and suspend disbelief, triggering the equivalent of a nuclear chain reaction, mushrooming through Canadian real estate.

Clearly, Ken LeBlanc and his PropertyGuys.com partners have done some serious splashing at their Waterslide Park, knowing that any business or career only ever grows to what can be imagined.

Can you suspend disbelief and start hurtling along a Waterslide of Imagination?

Is a new script waiting to be written for your brand?

Might want to get your popcorn ready.

"Logic will get you from Point A to Point B.
Imagination will take you everywhere."

-ALBERT EINSTEIN

2
To Brand or Not to Brand

"I don't know what it is but I remember when me and my buddies used to ride them Yamahas we'd go out on the road for days and no one would ever look twice or stop to talk to us. But, ever since we started drivin' Harley's, now it seems like at every truckstop or shopping mall, there is no shortage of folks who want to come up and start yakkin' with us about our hogs." -**H-D RIDER**

Marketing and advertising people tend to casually sprinkle the words "brand" and "branding" in many conversations – without listeners clearly understanding the precise meaning of those terms. But if you were to ask over a hundred different experts in the marketing and advertising arena to define their terminology, don't be surprised if you hear over a hundred different answers.

Just for fun, substantiate this theory yourself with a Google search. Here are some snippets of the thousands of definitions, floating around in cyberspace.

- "In a nutshell, branding is all about perception."
- "Branding is a way of helping non-knowledgeable customers make a low-risk buying decision for commodity product with little inherent differentiation."
- "A brand is the most valuable real-estate in the world, a corner of the consumer's mind."
- "The intangible sum of a product's attributes: its name, packaging, and price, its history, its reputation, and the way it's advertised."

Wikipedia defines "brand" as: *"A collection of experiences and associations attached to a company, product or service;*

specifically, concrete symbols such as a name, logo, and slogan and design scheme. A symbolic embodiment of all information connected to companies, products and services." Another Wikipedia incarnation distills it to: *"A collection of experiences and associations connected with a service, a person or any other entity."*

There you go. Clear as a Shakespearian sonnet.

But, wait ... there's more!

Would you believe the Direct Marketing Association Website has nearly 30 definitions of branding?

But, how does any reasonable business owner expect to develop a brand strategy, cut cheques for professional marketing services and implement a campaign without a clear definition to work from? This lack of clarity has created many misconceptions about what may be the most misinterpreted word in the business vocabulary: Brand.

Many people believe a "brand" is a product - something tangible you hold in your hand, drink, wear, or place on your foot. Or that "branding" equals advertising. Or that branding is marketing – and therefore the responsibility of the marketing department.

Karen Post - a.k.a. "The Branding Diva" – and author of *Brain Tattoos*, offers the following:

"A brand is a story, embedded in the mind of the market"

Repeated market testing reveals Karen's definition stands head and shoulders above all others and makes the most sense to business owners who are serious about growth. A "story" is an intangible. "Embedded" means the story has sunk in and sticks like glue in the brains of real people. And the "market"?

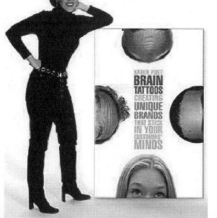

It consists of everyone - from paying customers to employees, new recruits, suppliers, and investors.

Why does this matter?

Just look up and down any grocery aisle and ask yourself what the difference is between national brands and the store or generic ones. According to Harry Beckwith, author of the best-seller, *Selling the Invisible*, store and generic brands own about 7% of any market while name brands account for the other 93%. Name brands charge about 40% more for their products and services, spend less time and money attracting new business, and in the case of Kraft Foods sell for about 8 times its book value. In other words, owning a brand of choice equals competitive advantage; increased sales, market share and overall profitability.

Look at brand "value" this way.

Water is a commodity. Readily available. It also happens to be FREE.

Water + Brand Name **(Evian)** = $1.50 / bottle.

Water + Brand Name **(Bling H2O)** + endorsed by Paris Hilton = $60.00 / bottle

Long before Joseph Pine and James Gilmore wrote their 1999 book, *The Experience Economy, Work is Theatre & Every Business a Stage,* Harley-Davidson had determined the value in creating a compelling brand story – a story filled with drama and a dream for its thrill-seeking customers.

One H-D senior exec was once quoted as saying, *"What we sell is the ability for a 55-year-old accountant to dress in black leather, ride through small towns and have people be afraid of him".* These merchants of menace figured out long ago exactly what they were selling through their bikes and merchandise – and precisely what their customer "from middle-class family man to hell-raising outlaw" was buying; the ability to become a character inside the drama of "riding the dream" - absolute freedom of expression on the open road.

Whether we ride a Harley, sip on a Starbucks latte or reassure ourselves with Dove Soap, is it really the product we're buying? Or are we buying the *feeling?* Great brands seamlessly infiltrate the heart and soul of consumers, busting through the advertising clutter by telling a better story. Speaking to us at primal levels, the best brands in the world are quietly marking their turf within our psyches.

"Though this be madness, yet there is method in 't."
-HAMLET(Act II, Scene II)

Once you have your story straight, so it clearly stands for something your customer would care about, only then can you Pass GO and digest the concept of brand<u>ing</u>; the tangible process of creating and managing signals to transmit the brand idea. That little "ing" makes a big difference.

"Branding" injects tangible elements and activities to communicate a "story" – everything from websites to washrooms; business cards to television and radio commercials; from wardrobe to the way the phone is answered. From that perspective, "seamless" branding becomes everyone's job. Front of the house. Back of the house. Not just the guy who writes the ads.

If you're worried your brand is much ado about nothing, you may want to revisit your company roots. Do an archeological dig. What did your business stand for originally? Why did it resonate with customers in the first place? Are the core values still relevant?

COLLECT
$200.00 SALARY
AS YOU PASS

GO

Some realities to consider:

1. Brands are about feelings not facts.
2. Brands make people decide things.
3. Brands create differentiation.
4. Brands generate greater profits.
5. Every business or person has a brand. Either by accident or design. And there is no "Get Out of Brand Free" card.

In the marketplace of the future, a compelling "story" will be the new currency - and the ability of a brand to inspire its followers will become increasingly vital in the quest for mind and market share. Will you learn to win hearts and souls before earning resumés or credit card numbers?

When your "story" begins to rev like the throaty rumble of a Harley V-Twin engine, supported by an organization that can deliver on a brand promise with integrity, you are on a fast-track to occupying and monopolizing a most favourable position in your market.

Clearly, your brand is not part of the business. It IS the business. And since every brand is a story and all the world's a stage, do you have a "hang on to your handlebars" type of story worth sharing?

A story an audience can believe in?

One that could kick start a tribe?

And leave it thirsting for more?

"To thine own self be true, and it must follow, as the night the day, thou canst not then be false to any man."

- WILLIAM SHAKESPEARE

3
Common Patterns, UnCommon Sense

Conventional wisdom dictates: *"Don't re-invent the wheel!"*

Conventional wisdom, however, is not necessarily true. And it often becomes your biggest hurdle to introducing new theories, concepts, and ideas. In reality, "conventional wisdom" is typically more conventional than wise – but how do you confront this obstacle and set your business and brand apart?

A good place to begin would be to search the pages of history to learn what other remarkable dreamers and achievers have already done. The automotive industry is a prime example.

More than a century ago, legions of horseless carriage builders sprang up in scattered backyards and barns throughout North America and Europe. For the better part of 30 years, people like Karl Benz assembled their products, one at a time (often by hand), bringing together wheels and axles, windshields and engine blocks - and everything in between. These products were then taken to market and sold to wealthy customers as high end luxuries. In those days, cars were generally expensive and difficult to maintain – and no fewer than 502 firms in the U.S. struggled between 1900 and 1908 to manufacture automobiles at a profit. One of the early casualties of this business model was Detroit Automobile Company. It went bankrupt in 1902 after selling fewer than half a dozen cars in two years, and firing its chief engineer.

Down, but by no means out, the unemployed engineer, knew there had to be a better way. A year later, Henry formed his own company and went looking for inspiration – outside his own industry. In Chicago he visited a slaughterhouse at the Union Stockyards – and he could not believe his eyes. Fate and

23

vision collided the very moment Henry saw the "disassembly line". Cattle being cut apart as the carcasses moved along a conveyor. Butchers on either side of the line removing the same body parts of a cow, over and over.

Henry could not help but notice a Common Pattern.

Suddenly, it was so easy to see what was flawed with the processes he and his competitors had been using for so long. In observing the processes of an industry/ discipline outside his own, Henry realized that the next step was to use UnCommon Sense and simply reverse the process in his own category.

By 1908, Henry's "Ford Motor Company" plant *Henry Ford* was turning out thousands of Model T's each month, leaving hundreds of Henry's competitors choking in the dust of his innovative thinking. Daring to dream in this lateral, horizontal fashion allowed Henry Ford to see what so many others had failed to. To paraphrase Thomas Edison, *"The world outside of your industry, market or profession is full of existing ideas that people have never fully capitalized upon, which may be adapted to your specific need or challenge"*. Vertical solutions or "best practices" are typically based on existing ideas or knowledge - solutions others have already experienced some success with - like drilling deeper into an existing oil well.

Thinking from a broader perspective allows you to ask different questions, ones that can stitch together, seemingly unrelated concepts, thoughts and ideas. Lateral, horizontal thinking can be compared to yeast. You don't need a lot but, you can't make bread or beer without it.

More often than not you will hear tired, familiar phrases expressed by those who naively believe their business model or brand can stand out in a crowd. In the advertising industry, for example, about 90% of the copy comes from recycling other ads. It doesn't take a lot in the way of creativity to suggest *"Why don't we say some of the same things our competitors are saying? Hey, if it's proven and it works ... Why re-invent the wheel?"*

This safe, logical, risk-free approach will have many vertical, linear thinkers nodding in agreement. But don't hold your breath waiting for these companies to become remarkable in anything they create or say. You can't expect to invent new products, services, techniques or develop a kick-ass brand promise and message without challenging fundamental assumptions about the business you are currently in. So rise to the challenge or resign yourself to a dreary fate of incremental improvements at best. And don't be surprised if and when you get blindsided by someone like Henry who decided to view things from a different, slightly haphazard, horizontal angle.

Could you take a panoramic view of industries or disciplines other than your own? Where could you apply horizontal thinking and discover Common Patterns that make UnCommon Sense? And envision windows that magically open in the movie theatre of your imagination?

Henry Ford is but one in a long line of visionary intuitive innovators who took time to notice what was going on around them. Fred Smith got the idea for FedEx and overnight delivery by noticing how banks processed and moved paperwork throughout their network. General Mills and Southwest Airlines spent countless hours watching and studying the pit crews of the Indy 500 to help improve turnaround times at manufacturing plants and airport terminals.

And the original McDonald brothers, Dick and Maurice borrowed Henry's production line concept to make burgers, shakes and fries in a more efficient manner before Ray Kroc came along in 1955 to sell them some milkshake machines. When the McDonald brothers were reluctant to expand beyond their neck of the woods, Ray eventually bought them out, franchised the idea and revolutionized the entire food service industry.

To discover UnCommon Sense for your business or career you will have to sit down, put yourself in park, and ponder these questions:

- *What is the specific challenge/problem I'm trying to solve?*
- *Who else - in a category or discipline other than my own - has successfully solved this issue?*
- *How did they solve it? What specific steps did they take?*
- *Can those steps be adapted to fit my situation?*

If these questions fail to produce answers, ask yourself:

- *How would a 6-year old look at this issue?*
- *What would a kid tell you to?*
- *Or how about a farmer, athlete, musician, cartoonist or street person?*

Answers to your biggest business or career issues could lie in many fields; an "Our Lady Peace" rock video, architectural design, military strategy, quantum physics, the animal kingdom and who knows where else? Imagine what breakthroughs you can discover by pinpointing principles, tested and proven in seemingly unrelated, but parallel worlds.

In my own case, an unexpected resource has been the enduring, fascinating and utterly addictive game of golf. Like the Game of Business, golf is a paradox - a contradiction between simplicity and complexity. The top pros in the world make it look so easy that you think you can do it. But you may have already discovered golf is not nearly as easy as it looks.

Let's start with simplicity.

Growing up as the son of a local club pro in Eastern Canada, a boy witnesses a timeless principle first hand:

"The ball is either in or out. Close doesn't count".

A three-inch putt is the same on a scorecard as a 300-yard drive.

Later in life, after making the transition from employee to entrepreneur, I couldn't help but notice obvious parallels and connections between golf and business. For example:

- Nothing happens in business without a sale.
- Unless there is a sale – there is no customer.
- Unless there is a customer – there is no business.

The complexity in both business and golf lies in execution and delivery. Like a business owner, whenever a golfer makes a mistake, there are no teammates to blame. Links can also be made between the focus, mental toughness and the need to apply fundamentals week after week on the tournament circuit are similar traits often attributed to extraordinary business leaders. Golfers also adapt to new courses and conditions that change constantly, recognizing they will only be compensated in direct proportion to the level of their performance. Anyone who competes on the playing field of 100% commission can make these mental connections easily.

Conventional wisdom stifles creativity, never allowing you to see possibilities and make connections buried in worlds other than your own.

Unconventional thinking allows you to soar with the eagles.

Do you see any lateral hazards and opportunities that exist in disciplines and industries outside your current realm? Think you could connect horizontal dots from unlikely fairways - seamlessly integrate them into your brand and business model - and then grip it and rip it?

What Common Patterns would make UnCommon Sense for you?

"If I had asked people what they wanted, they would have replied – faster horses."

- HENRY FORD

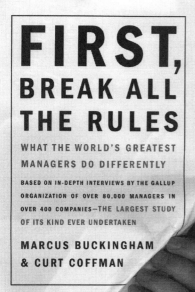

FIRST, BREAK ALL THE RULES

WHAT THE WORLD'S GREATEST MANAGERS DO DIFFERENTLY

BASED ON IN-DEPTH INTERVIEWS BY THE GALLUP ORGANIZATION OF OVER 80,000 MANAGERS IN OVER 400 COMPANIES—THE LARGEST STUDY OF ITS KIND EVER UNDERTAKEN

MARCUS BUCKINGHAM & CURT COFFMAN

Are there common patterns that make uncommon sense when it comes to leading people? Authors Marcus Buckingham and Curt Coffman reveal in First Break All the Rules, great managers share one common trait: They break virtually every "rule" held sacred by conventional wisdom. For example, they reject the idea that, with enough training, a person can do anything he sets his mind to. The best of 80,000 managers surveyed, don't try and "fix" weaknesses, and focus instead on the strengths already inside their people.

4
Purpose of a Business

It may be the most fundamental business question of all.

"What is the purpose of a business?"
Come again?
The purpose of a business???

No one understood the implications of this question with more clarity than Ted.

As a senior business professor at Harvard, Theodore Levitt had a reputation as a popular – but demanding - teacher. Classes were equal parts lecture and theatre. Sometimes he would toss chalk at blackboards – or occasionally at a student. In the *Harvard Business Review* Ted would provoke his readers to reexamine fixed points of view, compelling them to think more creatively. His 1960 manifesto, *"Marketing Myopia"* argued that companies should never define themselves by the products they sold - but rather by the customers they served. Levitt contended that that was why railroads ultimately lost the battle for passenger traffic to aviation – simply put: the rail barons failed to embrace the technology of flight to better serve its customers when it had more than enough financial, operational and human resources to do so.

"The railroads did not stop growing because the need for passenger and freight transportation declined. That grew. The railroads are in trouble today not because that need was filled by others (cars, trucks, airplanes, and even telephones) but because it was not filled by the railroads themselves. They let others take customers away from them because they assumed themselves to be in the railroad business rather than in the transportation business. They defined their industry incorrectly because they were railroad oriented instead of transportation oriented; product oriented instead of customer oriented"

-THEODORE LEVITT, 1960

Clearly, the Dukes of Diesel missed a flight filled with opportunity.

Now you know the real reason why we aren't flying on Reading, Union Pacific or CNR airlines instead of Continental, American Airlines or WestJet. Myopic vision and a lack of clarity could not keep rail firmly in the lead over upstart aviators despite having many more resources at their disposal. That's how Ted determined the only valid definition of business purpose:

"The Purpose of a Business is to Create & Keep a Customer."

Ask enough people the "purpose of a business" question over a decade and you will notice an unmistakable, chaotic pattern in their answers.

And while the answers aren't necessarily incorrect, they are, nonetheless, incomplete. Everyone in your business should on "the same page". After all, if there are discrepancies on how the question is viewed at the executive, management and front-line levels, brand disconnects become inevitable. Your business will lack direction and focus like a ship without a compass.

Answers to the question (What is the purpose of a business?) tend to fall into three categories. The first (and most frequent response) is that the purpose of a business is to make money. This premise, however, can often lead to a number of brand maladies including product centricity or, even worse, financial centricity. There is no denying revenue and profitability is essential for a business to survive and grow, but is that what the question was asking? Is profit really the Purpose of a business or is profit merely a Result of a business fulfilling its Purpose? Given that profits (and losses) are nothing more than forms of measurement, one can only conclude that in no way shape or form does Result resemble Purpose.

Others suggest that the purpose of a business is to satisfy customer needs. Doing what it takes to deliver products and services people will buy. But is that really the Purpose of a business or does this represent what a business does in Action form to fulfill its Purpose? Are Actions and Purpose the same thing?

A third response often heard is that the real purpose of a business is to give the owner of that business more freedom and control. Many do go into business with the goal of achieving something that fulfills their dreams, but is that really the Purpose of the business or of the Person who owns it? Are the business and the Person one and the same? If you accept the game of golf as a worthy metaphor, then these questions must be addressed in the same spirit as the ball being in or out. In business, we either make a sale or we don't. We either have a customer or we don't. Just as a proper grip is fundamental to a successful golf swing, so is clarity on this basic question of business purpose.

Think of "Create & Keep a Customer" as a principle you can always count on, in the same way ancient mariners relied on Polaris for nighttime navigation.

Without a North Star, sailors get lost.

Without a solid grip, golfers hook, slice, duff and curse.

Without "Create & Keep a Customer" many business owners will see their vision shrouded in the darkness of myth and misinformation.

Ted Levitt believed that without a customer, no business would be in a position to pay salaries dividends and taxes, employ people, or provide products and services. Without acquiring and keeping enough paying customers, there is no business.

Making money, delivering products and services and fulfilling individual hopes and dreams are the end results of a successful business and what its brand can deliver – not the driving mechanism.

Successful executives leading great brands, never lose sight of this.

Theodore Levitt went on to write that "Purpose of a Business" serves as the overarching principle that drives all other functions. Look at it this way:

1. Purpose of a Business = Create & Keep a Customer

2. Which means, the Business will need to Produce and Sell what a paying customer would actually want and/or value.

3. Which allows, the Business to generate positive cash flow, thus ensuring sustainability through continuous profitability. Revenues must exceed costs.

4. Which will rarely happen without a clear vision of company purpose and plans, who the business serves, how it is different and a well-founded strategy designed to attract customers.

5. Which then requires a well-designed Business System to keep those customers by ensuring what needs doing gets done – and when not, gets fixed.

Companies operating with a purpose primarily focused on money, activities or personal interests inevitably lose sight of the reasons why the business exists in the first place. Customers – both internal and external – often, unwittingly, wind up as mere cogs in a business machine, which is typically the last thing any thinking human would want. Essentially the "purpose" question identifies a clear difference between a philosophy that values transactions and results as opposed to one that values relationships and long-term growth.

How does this thinking square with your own in terms of your vision?

Does the Levitt definition give you a better handle on what your business is really all about? Can you see where Ted has made it easier for you to navigate the waters of business complexity?

And be ready to adjust when times and technology change?

For your business and brand to become "seamless", a clear definition of business purpose needs to be top of mind for everyone who buys into your vision. How much further ahead would your business be, if everyone connected to it could grasp this simple, yet powerful explanation of why a business exists in the first place?

How many misunderstandings could be avoided if people in your business understood the glaring difference between a shared common purpose as opposed to individual roles and responsibilities? Do the people you work with now understand the difference between their purpose and their job?

31

Are you getting a grip on the real reason "why" your business exists?

Once you fully grasp the "why", the "what we do" and "how we do it" becomes easier to identify and translate into action.

Do you think this might be one of the reasons why Starbucks, Apple and Southwest Airlines have done OK for themselves by figuring out they weren't in the "coffee", "computer" or "airline" business but in the "people" business?

Gripping the "What" & "How"

Since no two businesses or brands are identical, neither are the ways and means they employ to Create & Keep a Customer. Examining the Levitt definition at a deeper level allows you to see the implications.

Create = Branding, Marketing, Direct Selling, Public Relations, Advertising, Guerilla Marketing, Word-of-Mouth, Social Media, Networking, Location, etc.

Keep = Capacity/Inventory, Quality, Efficient Operations, Accounting, Talent-Fit, Recruiting, Hiring, Training, Innovation, Sustainable Model, Product or Service Diversification, "Customer Experience", Community Involvement, Leadership, Social Values, etc.

Customer = Internal/External, Asset/Liability, Gain/Pain

"The public be damned! The railroads are not run for the benefit of the 'dear public. That cry is all nonsense. They are built by men who invest their money and expect to get a fair percentage on the same."
- WILLIAM K. VANDERBILT, 1882

5
Creating & Keeping Customers

"I've been running businesses for more than thirty years and all this time, I just knew there had to be an easier way to explain what we were doing. Still can't believe it was that simple. This captures what I have felt all along."

The multi-millionaire who flew in for the off-site meetings was still wearing a look of amazement the next morning. Fuelled by a Tim Horton's coffee and Danish, the wheels were now turning at a furious pace in the mind of the man who owns 43 rust-proofing franchises. Now that he had gained clarity on WHY a business exists in the first place - to Create & Keep a Customer - his imagination was in Bachman-Turner Overdrive; ready to roll on down a highway of long-term profitability and success in his current and newest ventures.

Gaining clarity on the Purpose of a Business - to Create & Keep a Customer- allowed him to break free from theoretical clutter and focus on a timeless, principle that would serve as a foundation for his different business models.

Clarity - the unvarnished truth – has a way of doing that.

Dazed and confused no longer, the wealthy man leaned forward, insistent, "Tell me more!"

No problem.

Once business purpose has been clearly defined, you can now start asking better questions about how this applies to you. First, it will typically cost your business 5-to-10 times more to create a

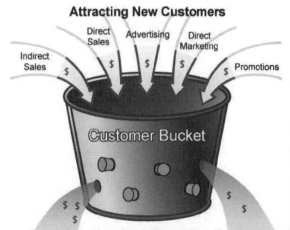

new customer than to keep an existing one. In his book, *"The Loyalty Effect"*, author Frederick Reichheld contends even a 5% increase in customer retention drives a 25-to-100% increase in profitability.

Plug the leaks.

Focus on retention.

Watch profits grow.

Strategically, this is the long-term approach for those who are serious about "seamless" brand-building.

It is not a strategy recommended for fast-buck, quick-change, artists.

In terms of actually taking care of business, there are many different methods and tactics used to "Create". Everything from direct mail, radio ads and cold-calling, to guerrilla marketing, television, social media and word-of-mouth. And because no two businesses are exactly the same, the approach should be specific to your model and the customers it serves. For example, a business with few competitors in a high traffic area could spend very few advertising dollars, relying instead on architectural word-of-mouth as the way to be noticed. Picture a gas station with a WWII fighter on the roof or a roadside fruit and vegetable stand, fronted by a grinning, giant potato. One of the best examples is the Irving Mainway station outside of Nackawic, New Brunswick. It boasts the presence of the world's largest axe. Of course people are tempted to pull over and take a second, closer look. And now that they're stopped anyways – why not fill up the gas tank and buy a coffee?

Customer retention – the "Keep"- is a different story altogether. You have to consider functions and activities that range from operational systems, product quality, staffing, accounting practices and inventory management, to the "experience" your company actually delivers to the end user. It's a lot easier to make a customer promise than to keep one.

The "Keep" depends on you.

And your ability to manage and lead people - organize and implement systems – and consistently communicate and innovate.

There is little glamour in the "Keep" side of your business as you ensure the "guts" of HR and Operations are aligned with the "glory" of marketing. Yet, this is the area of greatest focus for brands like WestJet who recognize creating an environment that encourages employee engagement is what drives its culture of retention; attracting and keeping the best front-line people in turn inspires customer loyalty.

Finally, have you thought about the type of "Customer" you want your brand to attract?

Customers will always fall into one of two categories.

External customers who fork over dollars for your product or service.

Internal customers – employees who represent your brand and deliver – or fail to deliver - on its promises.

Internal customers and the impact they have on your business is critical – which is why shaping your business into a great place to work is vital. Employee turnover can be expensive and exhausting. The figures speak for themselves: If a minimum wage employee leaves after just three months on the job, real and hidden costs work out to about $4000. Internal and external customers can be categorized as either assets or liabilities. Ask yourself; is this customer – internal or external - a plus or a minus? A gain or a drain?

If you want your business and brand to be "seamless", you must nurture your customers to the point where they become:

- Loyal and raving fans.
- Your very own brand ambassadors.
- A free sales and recruitment force – at no cost to you.

This "seamless" formula for excellence, flowing from the "Create and Keep a Customer" model - is understood and applied by many leading brands such as WestJet, Harley-Davidson, Starbucks, Apple, and Disney.

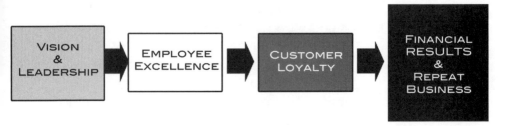

VISION & LEADERSHIP → EMPLOYEE EXCELLENCE → CUSTOMER LOYALTY → FINANCIAL RESULTS & REPEAT BUSINESS

"It's easy to have a cheerful, helpful and motivated cast member when he or she comes right out of the 'Traditions' class at Disney University. The challenge is to keep that person motivated six months later when it's 90 degrees with 98% humidity. The answer is not constant training. The answer is leadership."

- JAYNE PARKER, Disney University

Are customers in love with your brand?

Or are they just "satisfied"?

A Vanderbilt University study once revealed 25-40% of "satisfied" customers may not come back. Gallup studies indicate only 29 percent of employees in the United States are fully engaged in their work.

Most customers – internal or external - are neither big fans nor ruthless opponents.

Most customers are simply indifferent.

And nothing will kill a business with deadly effectiveness like indifference.

Studies have revealed 96% of dissatisfied customers will never complain. If they did, you might have a chance to rectify the situation. But they don't. Typically, a disheartened customer – internal or external - will quietly depart and shop or work elsewhere. As American playwright Clare Booth Luce put it, "There is nothing harsher than the softness of indifference."

Customer satisfaction is sending a happy customer OUT of your business; customer loyalty is bringing a happy customer BACK. Today's satisfied customer becomes your competitor's satisfied customer - tomorrow. Unless you start going to war and battling for the customers you really want.

Given that good service and fair pay are expected as a matter of course, why not do the unexpected?

Could you do something outrageous that turns your customer into a walking, talking advertisement? How about, if you owned a restaurant, giving everyone in your restaurant a gift card instead of a bill, randomly one night per month. How would you react if that happened to you? How many friends would you tell? And how many of them would be tempted to visit that restaurant? Fifty percent? Eighty percent? What would be the impact on a keen golfer who decides to ante up for a membership? Imagine his or her delight when, out of the blue, a box of Nike golf balls arrives with a handwritten note from the club pro saying, "Thanks for becoming a member, we really appreciate it". And can you imagine how a faithful hard-working employee would feel if her boss walked in unannounced and handed over a new Nintendo Wii to bring home to the kids? Consider the impact that gesture would have on a single mom suffering from the guilts of last Christmas when Santa couldn't deliver what the kids really wanted under the tree.

There are hundreds of outrageous ideas you can dream up to create and keep customers – both external and internal - customers who would love to jump in and share a foxhole with your brand.

What new ways can you start *"Takin' Care of Business"*?

Before departing the offsite meeting later that afternoon, the owner of more than 40 franchise units and several other companies was in high gear, revving his idea motor with how he would attack his new list of priorities.

With renewed confidence and a fresh sense of clarity, he shook hands, looked his hosts square in the eye and uttered, *"You ain't seen nothin' yet"*.

"When you get successful, you can do pretty much whatever you want."

- RANDY BACHMAN

6
A Love Story

New Brunswick's provincial capital provides an unlikely setting for a story that may tug on your heartstrings. Home of both St. Thomas University and the University of New Brunswick, Fredericton is an epicentre of government power and academia. The kind of place where big thinkers and even bigger talkers come together.

Several years ago, I found myself addressing a Fredericton Chamber of Commerce breakfast meeting at the Lord Beaverbrook Hotel. About 60 people showed up for a program on Sales Strategies for Small Business. After I finished, there was a scattering of people who came over and offered thanks before quickly bidding farewell as they rushed off to other, more important stuff in their day. But, out of the corner of my eye, I noticed two gentlemen patiently standing at the back of the room. Waiting to get a word in edgewise.

The older of the two was a polite, shy sort, mid-to- late 40's minus the middle age spread. Jim introduced himself and his colleague – a late 20's man with a quick smile – offered profuse thanks for the presentation and asked about sales training possibilities for his staff at the used car dealership he owned and operated on the north side of town.

Then he handed me his business card.

At first glance, there was something about the card that struck me. And it had nothing to do with the design, logo, or colours - which were ordinary at best. Not a card that would earn a spot in the Visual Branding Hall of Fame. But there was this one quirky phrase, a quote that read:

> *"The glow of one warm thought is, to me,*
> *worth more than anything. Thank You".*

Hmm. "That's different", I thought. "Even a little 'out there'. Not something you expect to see from a guy selling used cars".

I mentioned that I had some time early that afternoon before heading back home, so I could drop in on his shop. We parted ways. I headed off to a previously scheduled meeting and around one o'clock, crossed the Westmorland Street Bridge to visit Jim Gilbert's Wheels & Deals.

With no idea of what was in store.

"Not a bad looking building, clean, organized. Tasteful ceramic tile flooring. There seems to be a lot of those Successories motivational plaques everywhere; on walls, desks, counters. Not what I expected. Interesting."

I sat down in a neatly appointed office and within minutes a certain spirit and warmth was oozing out of Jim as he gushed openly about his admiration for people like Tony Robbins, Brian Tracy, Zig Ziglar, and others. The shyness disappeared as Gentleman Jim shared his vision of what he wanted his dealership to be and in that quiet, humble voice of his, as he explained to me what he valued most, he said something about his business philosophy that I have never forgotten to this day.

"It's not about Four Wheels and a Piece of Tin"

He explained how every one of his competitors had "four wheels and a piece of tin" but that he wanted his focus to be entirely different. He talked about how he really cared about his customers and wanted his sales staff to care just as much - if not more. He explained all the things he did to raise the standards of the vehicles before they appeared on the lot - and how he took care of folks after the sale. He wanted to do business with people who would be so well served they would want to come back for their next purchase. And they would also tell their friends. So that day, Jim and I started working together. I introduced a consultative training process for his sales team – three full-time and one part-time guy. Before long we were doing other things with his small group - using psychometric assessments to improve team dynamics for example - and then one day Jim asked about my business card.

He liked what he saw. The colours. The feel. He asked, "Who designed this?"

That's when I introduced Jim to one of our team members, who travelled to Fredericton and learned that Jim was a fan of Original Six hockey teams, Harley-Davidson motorcycles and Elvis - among other things. Jim also explained what he envisioned for Wheels & Deals and our guy went to work.

This is what he came back with.

Jim was jumping for joy! Someone had finally captured the essence of what his business was all about, in a way that he was proud to share with the rest of the world. And boy, has he been sharing, plastering the distinctive winged wheel on all manner of branding paraphernalia. Widely recognized all over the Fredericton area, Jim has used this logo as the visual anchor for a branding strategy that has caused customer heads to turn and competitors to grumble.

Knowing it was never about *"Four wheels and a piece of tin"*, Jim set about building a brand identity that would speak to the type of customers he cared about, instead of pushing transactional hunks of rubber and metal. The campaign was accelerated in September of 2006 as Jim Gilbert's Wheels & Deals became forever branded as "Canada's Huggable Car Dealer" with catchy radio vignettes sharing stories about the "Romeo of Roadsters", the "McDreamy of Drive" and the need for a daily shot of "Hugtonium". Gone are ads spewing white noise about makes, models and financing options, because after all ...

"It's not about Four Wheels and a Piece of Tin"

Jim also realized that you couldn't just talk about being "huggable" on the radio without backing that up with a "huggable" experience. As soon as you walk in the showroom and get a whiff of the free popcorn, see branded teddy bears in every vehicle, the state of the art video system, and the fireplace, nacho and espresso bar, you know this is unlike any other car dealership you have ever walked into.

Over the last several years Jim Gilbert has transformed an otherwise ordinary used car dealership into a memorable brand experience. A brand experience that has seen his company capture many business awards, attract newspaper and media attention and become recognized as an industry leader. His business has grown substantially, a new service centre has been added and what was once a small team of about 7 or 8 employees has grown into a healthy, vibrant company of 30-plus. He has even launched his own Internet television channel and a program called *"Motorvationally Speaking"*, to promote inspirational "fuel for thought" while showcasing other dreamers and achievers.

Jim humbly thanks a number of mentors who helped lift Wheels & Deals to the next level, but I think we can all learn so much more from him. There are few business owners who believe as much in the value of personal and professional development – and back it up with action. Jim constantly invests in staff training, even to the point of making sure each team member has a copy of Jack Mitchell's book, *"Hug Your Customers"*. Jim went the extra (thousand) miles to jump on his Harley and travel to meet the author in person so he could better explain the concepts to his front-line people. He has even trained his salespeople, who were initially reluctant, in the fine art of reaching out for a hug - but only when a customer is absolutely ready to receive one.

The Wheels & Deals team has learned (especially John!) that if they have an opportunity to "hug" a customer, it is very difficult for that person to walk down the street, kick tires and compare prices on somebody else's lot, because as Jim explains, *"It's not about Four Wheels and a Piece of Tin"*

What goes on in your business each day?

Do you have anything equivalent to "Four Wheels and a Piece of Tin" at your company? Is your primary focus on the "product" you sell? Or are you directing your energies towards the person who really sits in the driver's seat?

When was the last time you pondered how your business could impact the way a Customer actually feels? Ever stopped to consider the lifetime value of a single Customer? Or the number of referrals they generate because you dared to deliver your promise straight from the heart? What would it mean to the future growth of your business if Customers were coming back a second, third or fourth time because they knew you sincerely valued them?

For nearly three decades, Jim's heart was in the right place - long before he became a local celebrity of sorts - packaged and branded as "Canada's Huggable Car Dealer". The generous and caring spirit of what has become a great small business brand was there the day we met. Jim's quirky business card offered a hint of things to come:

**"The glow of one warm thought is, to me,
worth more than anything. Thank You."**

Your company may face many of the same competitive issues as Jim Gilbert's. And it's all too easy to fall into the same trap of doing what everyone else in your domain does. It takes a brave individual to venture out to the skinny part of the branch and call himself "huggable". But no one ever reaches the fruit by playing it safe. And being boring just might be the riskiest strategy of all.

In business - as in life - we get what we focus on.

What is your business – and by extension your brand – focused on?

"If we don't take care of our customers, someone else will" **- UNKNOWN**

Side Two

7. Disconnected Brand Disorder

8. High Voltage Branding

9. Four Strong Winds

10. Wheels on Your Bus

11. From a Wrench to a Wiki

12. Brand Runner

13. A Phone Call to Phil

14. Burning the Boats

15. A Tale of Two Airlines

16. Selling Your "Soap"

"But I believe we have a higher level of mentality within us, but we have to use the power in the right way" **- TINA TURNER**

7
Disconnected Brand Disorder

Driving along Main Street, my 20-something son notices a 30-foot billboard.

"For Guys Who Don't Dance" is the message advertised by a national billiards franchise. Without missing a beat, Ryan exclaims, "That's the kind of place for me. To hell with that techno-disco scene with that loud thumping. Forget "Night at the Roxbury". Give me a place where I can kick back, relax, enjoy some suds and chat without having to scream over the racket."

Ten minutes later, on the other side of town, we pass a franchise location sporting a huge banner advertising "Friday Night Dance Party with DJ Dave".

Wait a second.

Isn't this the same franchise?

In the same city?

Are they sending two entirely different messages? Or are we missing something?

It would appear making a promise is one thing but keeping it is a challenge for this particular franchise. A classic case of Disconnected Brand Disorder - when advertising and actions don't quite match up.

Plastering one message on a 30-foot billboard and delivering something else to your customer could be symptomatic of any number of issues. Signals get crossed and Disconnected Brand Disorder ensues when companies have Sales, Operations and HR pursuing strategies in isolation from what Marketing may be working on. Disconnected Brand Disorder reveals itself in many forms - an insidious condition preventing companies and their people from reaching their full potential.

Effective branding - the ultimate business strategy - stems not from ads, products, and services - but from what a business stands for. A brand uncertain about that stance, unclear about its very reason for being, will fall for anything - wasting time, energy, money and other resources, scrambling to find short-term marketing, HR and operational band-aids.

Have you noticed one or more of the following?

Common Symptoms of Disconnected Brand Disorder

- Customer Apnea
- "Spray & Pray" Fever
- Hiring by Injection
- Integrity Influenza
- Marketing Measles
- Vision Impaired

Customer Apnea: *"Take a number..."*

How many companies are asleep at the wheel with the way transactions are handled? Many opportunities to build brand loyalty are missed at the front line by people who won't look you in the eye, smile or do anything to make you feel the least bit welcome. A monotone grunt that sounds like "Next" does nothing to make you feel better about the transaction that just took place. Worse  is when dial into any leviathan corporation and get lost in the telephone matrix - a maze of disconnected departments. With each call transfer, you repeat the same story, hoping each time that you are finally speaking to a real person who can actually resolve your issue.

When a fully alert brand delivers an eye-popping experience, we adopt it as our own. Some brands generate so much loyalty that you take mental ownership, saying things like "That's my coffee shop", "That's my banker", "That's my stylist". When we feel positive vibes with a brand and its people, we reward them with loyalty and repeat business. Typically, for every person that has a good experience with a brand they are likely to tell three others - but for every negative experience, they'll share it with ten or twelve. Somewhere out there, one company in your category may wake up and smell the brand experience coffee; greeting customers by name, guiding (not pointing) them to their destination, limiting the length of checkout lines, solving problems outside of voicemail jail and making sure customers always feel valued.

"Spray & Pray" Fever: *"We just need more traffic ..."*

Don't you just jump for joy when generic newsletters arrive from banks, credit card, insurance and real estate companies? If this tree-killing approach rarely, if ever, works on you, what would make you think your customer will buy into any form of advertising carpet-bombing? Typically, mass media formats like direct mail, newspapers and others capitalize on a business owners desire to be instantly gratified. That's why media reps can convince decision-makers to hand over cash for generic "white noise" that gets pumped into the $300 billion dollar North American advertising industry – whether it works or not. To do so otherwise would be to risk trying something new. Being different. Like crafting messages with considerably more mental traction than *"Quality, Selection and Everyday Low Prices from Fast, Friendly and Knowledgeable Staff!"*

It takes much more effort (not to mention courage) to construct a message your customer will actually care about. But, it's much safer, easier and there's more false sense of security in doing what has always been done to generate customer "traffic".

Hiring by Injection: *"Two Feet & a Heartbeat"*

Have you ever yet heard a company say that they don't want to hire the best people? But how many truly walk that talk when you see hiring models based on a philosophy of "Spaghetti Recruiting". "Keep throwing enough shit at the wall and see what sticks". Call centres and fast-food joints are notorious for just wanting "bums in the seats". The result of this thinking often manifests in soaring turnover rates, plummeting morale, and frequent brand disconnects.

Hiring decisions directly impact an organization's control of its brand. Treat those decisions in a casual, loosey-goosey manner and you can expect the same in return. No organization can do better than the level of talent on the team. This is where a genuine approach, supported by a systemized process, can prevent turnover addicts from repeatedly rolling up their sleeve and jabbing themselves senseless. To kick this habit, tough questions must be asked: "What do our positions have to be to attract the kind of people we want?" "Where do we find those people?" "How do we get them interested?" and "What do we have to do – besides pay them - to keep our people interested and motivated?"

Marketing Measles: *"That looks OK ...let's go with that."*

Visual identity is a cornerstone of any branding initiative. Why then are spotty inconsistent images the norm in many organizations, confusing customers and undermining brand strength? No one can argue against the power of symbols and how they have influenced behaviour throughout the course of human history. Before humans could read or write, they could understand what a symbol stood for. Some have even suggested the development of logos parallels the rise of free enterprise.

When it comes to presenting a cohesive brand image, little things don't mean a lot - they mean everything. Logos. Colours. Graphics. Fonts. These are essential elements that, when applied across the board, prevent fragmented perceptions of what your brand symbolizes. A well-managed visual identity, resistant to individual tampering and tinkering, becomes the basis for making the most of each first and lasting impression.

Vision Impaired: *"Profit before Purpose"*

Profit is the lifeblood of any enterprise. Without it, the organism shrivels and eventually dies. However, profit is always the result of a brand's greater purpose (creating and keeping customers), as opposed to its driving mechanism. Visions based primarily on the profit motive always manifest in customers and employees becoming cogs in a machine, devoid of any genuine, human connection.

A car or a cup of coffee; a bicycle or a salad bowl; any product or service can easily become just another commodity in the mind of your customer. When that happens, the only way for companies to compete is on price. A game where low price  wins in a downward spiral of lower profit margins driven by a legion of bargain-hunting, coupon-clipping, penny-pinching customers.

Legendary brands like Porsche and Starbucks refuse to play in that arena. Instead, they leverage brand as a differentiator. In the words of long-time Porsche CEO Peter Schutz, *"We're not selling cars. We're selling a dream"*. Starbucks, the Seattle-based java juggernaut brands itself less about coffee and more about being the inviting "third place" between work and home. As CEO Howard Schultz once explained, *"Starbucks provides much more than the best cup of coffee—we offer a community gathering place where people come together to connect and discover new things"*.

Integrity Influenza: *"Say One Thing ... Do Another"*

The source of brand strength is trust. The relationships you have with customers and employees are based on a foundation of trust. The trust then generates all of the other warm-and-fuzzy feelings of love, loyalty and desire. And nothing undermines brand strength quicker than hollow promises backed by zero intention of being kept.

Once upon a time, in the Kingdom of Radio, a company posted a plaque on the wall for all of the serfs, in all 24 locations to see. The barons who owned this broadcasting business must have been under the impression that these sacred words, covenants of a worthy mission, would serve as timeless scrolls to

48

inspire the salaried citizenry under their domain.

"We strive to be the most progressive broadcasting company in Canada, by providing high quality, local service to our listeners, achieving a measurable difference for our advertisers, rewarding the excellence of our employees and ensuring long term prosperity of our shareholders."

Within minutes of the plaques being posted throughout the land, employees were secretly pointing, giggling and chortling with each other. *"Yeah right. Who do they think they're trying to fool? High quality service? Rewarding excellence? About as likely as a buffalo flying out my butt. What a joke!"* Clearly, the emperors were not wearing any credible clothes with their employees. They had just called attention to the fact that they were dreadful at dealing with people. So terrible in fact that the company later became embroiled in several highly-publicized court cases (losing every one) involving the dismissal of popular personalities - at great cost to their brand both internally and externally.

Customers and employees hunger for truth. Because of this, Disconnected Brand Disorder – in all of its various forms - is easily diagnosed.

And you won't have to look far to find it.

You've been to the "typical" video store at one time or another.

These stores have the regular assortment of action/comedy/drama/kids videos in the front, but they also do brisk business from videos "out in the back". Often, these selections can be found in an isolated room just behind the swinging saloon doors, out back near the restrooms.

A room with shelves stocked full of adult videos.

This thread is not intended to debate moral arguments with respect to porn and whether or not store owners have a right to turn a profit. But, what if the store in question has a sign out front proudly calling itself "Family Video"?

Can you ever see this conversation unfolding?

"Honey, why don't you and the kids pick up a copy of 'Spiderman III', make sure you get them a computer game and while you're grabbing a chick flick, I'll just mosey on over to the

back of the store and get us 'The Best of Jenna & Friends' for later."

Purely from a branding perspective, you would be on safe ground with any number of company names; All-Star Video, Super Video, Video World, Video Village, Acme Video, etc., but do you see the irony and brand disconnect when a business trumpeting itself as "Family Video" features a XXX porn section?

Unfortunately, it's far from rare.

How many people have experienced other "typical" brand disconnects with any of the major cable or credit card companies? Have you noticed how these companies spend millions on advertising each year, but, will rarely think twice about allowing their brand to be destroyed by overzealous billing departments? It happens whenever a customer who fails to pay a monthly bill for the first time in 10 years, winds up with a threatening phone call or worse, a letter taped to the front door.

"Pay up within 72 hours or we will terminate your service!"

You would think a decade or more of paying bills on time would deserve a little latitude and a friendlier touch, however, stories like this are commonplace. It's unfortunate and ultimately frustrating, but far too often, marketing departments and ad agencies are isolated from the other parts of the business. Internal departments focus on internal problems – and forget the impact they can have on external brand perceptions, unwittingly creating various forms of Disconnected Brand Disorder.

Seamless branding is the process of aligning the behaviour of every component of an organization with the brand strategy. It reaches beyond marketing and advertising to include areas such as product design, packaging, customer service, sales, hiring practices, training, distribution channels, social media, the company name, logo and yes, even accounts receivable.

Like most powerful ideas, seamless branding is not overly complex - but not easy to accomplish. Often, the diverse, internal departments in many companies fail to grasp (or haven't been trained) that branding IS their business. The good news is that there is plenty of room at the top for companies that can successfully bring every part of the business into alignment around the brand promise. Everything that affects the customer experience - from websites to washrooms, from radio spots to front line reception, from customer service to signage - needs to be aligned.

It's been tough watching how the billiards franchise we talked about earlier has struggled in recent years. Head office has been forced to close down its flagship store and some support staff let go in an effort to stop the bleeding. Clearly, a billboard proclaiming one thing while a storefront banner advertises another is merely masking other, more serious vision & leadership issues that marketing band-aids can't repair.

Would you invest ad dollars just to drive customers to a Disconnected Brand?

Why spend a nickel on advertising unless you can be sure that the customers you most desire will arrive at a business ready to welcome them with a "seamless" experience? Can you see how you can actually shoot your brand in the foot (ouch!) by firing off advertising messages not supported or reinforced by what happens at the point of customer contact?

Disconnected Brand Disorder requires zero effort, planning or design. All you have to do is fail to develop or adhere to brand standards. Make sure to alienate or confuse core customers with mixed messages. Don't place any expectations of performance on staff or make a serious attempt to find and keep the good ones. And whatever you do, do not – repeat, do not - share your vision with your employees or educate and train them on the importance of brand values. Hey, what they know won't hurt them.

Brands are created intentionally or accidentally.

Is your brand strategy clear enough to guide all aspects of your organizational behaviour? Is your brand story being told in a consistent, seamless fashion, accurately describing what your company is all about and how it is different from your competitors? Would you believe that the cost of getting this wrong is typically much higher than the investment of doing it right?

Disconnected Brand Disorder comes with a price tag all its own.

One not easily measured.

Brands based solely on a 'profit motive' foundation miss out on possibilities that exist when a brand is centred on a compelling story that inspires trusting, long-term relationships with real human beings.

Your customers and employees are yearning to be part of something bigger; something to sustain them past the Friday Night Dance.

They're not really paying attention to what you say.

They're watching closely to see what you do.

"A lot of people just see this sex symbol, but I'm a pretty normal person and you'll find out I'm honestly just like the girl next door - well, the girl next door gone bad"

-JENNA JAMESON

8
High Voltage Branding

What does an arena rock band known as the "Thunder from Down Under", share in common with exceptional branding strategies?

Stick this story in your mental fuse box. See if you can detect the common patterns, the parallel principles of greatness in both sight and sound.

Like a killer song that keeps humming in your head, the words of Ryan Maxwell often echo in the neural chambers of anyone who has ever attended one of his riveting presentations on how to create show-stopping visual brands. With a speaking style imbued with mild shades of Ron Burgundy and Dr. Evil, this national award-winning art director enlightens and entertains audiences as he details what separates the top from the slop when it comes to eye-arresting commercial design.

Ryan, who has already racked up a number of brand portfolio chart-toppers, captures the essence of visual branding this way:

"Great design and great visual branding is actually very simple. Decide on a few basic rules - and stick to them"

Ryan explains that clear distinctions and decisions have to be drawn on choices that include fonts, colours, shapes and other key elements that determine whether your visual brand gets noticed. Once those choices have been made, your brand has an opportunity to become visually consistent, regardless of the marketing and promotional vehicles selected. As Ryan puts it, "Far better to invest time and energy up front to figure out what's going to last over the long haul. That way you're not always going back to the drawing board."

Recently, while on a midnight ride back from Fredericton, rocking out to the sounds of *"Black Ice"*, commonalities were coming on like a hurricane.

"Decide on a few basic rules - and stick to them"

Holy Hells Bells!

Isn't that how a scruffy bunch of Aussie rockers built and sustained one of the top music brands in the world?

Did they not lay down some basic rules that served as signposts on the long way to the front of the rock and roll train?

The story of AC/DC follows two tracks - the gradual evolution of a band that emerged as a leader in its genre - as well as the creation of a profitable business empire. Since their formation in 1973, AC/DC's commercial success flies in the face of conventional music industry wisdom. Founded by brothers Malcolm and Angus Young, the band has a reputation of being business savvy and a tendency of skipping an easy paycheque to preserve its long-term interests. AC/DC does not sell music online. They have never put out a greatest hits collection. Other musicians are not allowed to sample its songs. The band has also been reluctant to license its music for advertising.

If anyone could conduct a seminar on Brand Longevity, it would be Malcolm, Angus and their chord-crunching cohorts who continue to build a growing legion of rabid fans with the 2008 release of *"Black Ice"*, their first album in eight years. The AC/DC "formula" has provided enough creativity within structure to allow for more than three decades of loud, blistering hard rock that sells out giant football stadiums in minutes with millions of hard-core fans gobbling up merchandise by the truckload. The band has sold around 200 million albums worldwide, including more than 70 million in the US, where their seminal album Back in Black has sold more than 42 million copies alone.

The basic rules of this tried and tested "formula" include:

- Lead guitarist Angus Young, dressed in schoolboy attire, brandishing his trusty Gibson SG and doing the Chuck Berry duck walk. A whirlwind of on-stage kinetic energy which is only magnified by the relatively stationary, laid-back positions taken by his more reserved band mates.

- Lead singer Brian Johnson, a drinking buddy for "everyman", adorned with his standard "good ole bloke" flat cap.

- Rhythm guitarist Malcolm Young and bassist Cliff Williams, jeans and t-shirts guys who march straight up to their microphones to deliver background vocals - and march right back again. No muss. No fuss.

- Drummer Phil Rudd who refuses to fill any AC/DC track with any drum rolls, preferring instead to keep a steady, no-nonsense beat. (Rudd is rarely compared to drumming virtuosos like Deep Purple's Ian Paice or Neil Peart of Rush, but maybe that's not the purpose of the chain-smoking, stick-swinger behind the AC/DC drum kit).

- In terms of song-writing structure and production, you won't find AC/DC employing acoustic guitars, keyboards, synthesizers, techno beats or female voices. Power ballads, politically-charged anthems, unplugged sets and Celine Dion duets fall way outside the basic rules - NEVER part of the AC/DC brand mix.

Within the framework of this foundation, AC/DC carved out a reputation second to none in its genre, so much so that its brand strength has allowed it to make bold business decisions impacting the bottom-line in a big way. Upon its release, "Black Ice," hit Number One in 29 countries, including the U.S. (only available at Wal-Mart). Together, Columbia Records and Wal-Mart created a "Rock Again AC/DC Store" within all of its locations across America, marking the first time in history where Wal-Mart reserved such a large retail space to celebrate the release of a new album. The band also opted not to allow the album to be sold on iTunes. Critics of the Wal-Mart-only strategy were eating their words as over five million copies of "Black Ice" were shipped out in the first month alone.

"Decide on a few basic rules - and stick to them."

This formula has worked "seamlessly" for more than 30 years for AC/DC and their customer base has expanded in a way few would have predicted when they burst on to the scene in the early-to-mid 1970's with classics such as *"High Voltage"*, *"TNT"* and *"Dirty Deeds Done Dirt Cheap"*. Brand strength allowed AC/DC to withstand an eight-year recording and touring hiatus, while the ranks of its massive audience continued to swell as teenagers discovered the band through file sharing. Over dinner one night, I asked my 11-year old nephew, proudly displaying his *"Back in Black"* t-shirt what makes AC/DC so special, to which he replied, "They're unlike any other band out there today."

Consider for a moment:
- AC/DC gets less media hype than many acts it outsells.
- AC/DC never serves as gossip column fodder.
- AC/DC gets less airplay than Aerosmith, Britney or Celine.
- AC/DC has never been a favourite among critics.
- AC/DC has never pretended to anything but what they are.
- AC/DC sticks to what they know and do well.

Logos, design and other branding elements are as important in music as they are in clothing, consumer goods and the car business. Your business may not rack up numbers on the scale of a Nike or Nissan, but that doesn't mean your brand is any less important. The key is presenting a visual identity that people will notice and associate with your business. However, it must be noted: If AC/DC was a terrible band, the logo and brand identity would mean zilch. A logo means jack squat without the sound to shake it up and put it down.

"Ridin' down the highway, goin' to a show, stop in all the by-ways, playin' rock 'n' roll. Gettin' robbed. Gettin' stoned. Gettin' beat up. Broken boned. Gettin' had, gettin' took, I tell you folks, it's harder than it looks. It's a long way to the top if you wanna rock 'n' roll" **-BON SCOTT (1957-1980)**

When the Brothers Young started in Sydney, nobody knew who AC/DC were. They scratched and clawed their way along their personal and professional Highways to Hell to create a branding juggernaut perfectly designed to sell.
"Decide on a few basic rules - and stick to them."
What unshakable, no-compromise rules could you establish

as philosophical and visual foundations for your business, brand and career?

Can you establish a rock-solid essence and stick to certain basics that will sustain generations of societal and technological change, allowing your brand to remain relevant and leave customers thunderstruck for decades?

What is it in the AC/DC approach that could amplify your business or career and make the money talk?

Flick the switch.

Plug into high voltage branding.

"There are all sorts of cute puppy dogs, but it doesn't stop people from going out and buying Dobermans."
- ANGUS YOUNG

9
Four Strong Winds

Historically, this might be the original "seamless" brand.

"Seamless Brand"; defined as an organization that makes and keeps a promise that matters, through a business model that maintains consistent authenticity and delivery in key areas of Marketing, Human Resources and Operations.

To earn that distinction, a "seamless brand" must be who they say they are (in their marketing) and do what they say they'll do (internally with their people and the way customers are served). And for more than three decades, one company, above all others, has emerged as the undisputed leader in the "seamless" category.

And to think it all started on the back of a napkin.

This organization is consistently named among the top five Most Admired Corporations in America in Fortune magazine's annual poll. It is also:

- The largest airline in the world by number of passengers carried.
- Maintaining the 5th-largest passenger fleet of aircraft among all of the world's commercial airlines, with 3,500 flights daily.
- Serving twice as many customers per employee as any other airline.
- One of the world's most profitable airlines, posting a profit for the 35th consecutive year in January 2008.

Growing from just three planes and 250 people when it started, Southwest Airlines has been a trendsetter ever since. It introduced the first profit-sharing plan in the U.S. airline industry in 1973. Southwest consistently receives the lowest ratio of complaints per passengers boarded of all major U.S. carriers. It was one of the first airlines to recognize the value of "creating an environment" to foster a vibrant internal culture – which in turn created a distinct competitive advantage.

Put Southwest under the microscope of the "seamless" framework, and you feel the uplifting impact of four strong winds blowing in distinctly different directions. Evidently, those winds were felt as far away as Alberta in the mid-1990s, when WestJet Airlines practiced the sincerest form of flattery, imitating much of the successful Southwest model.

Here is a closer look at that framework:

EXTERNAL BRAND: Displaying the Promise

The fleet at Southwest Airlines boasts what some would consider the ugliest paint schemes known to man; but, as Herb Kelleher explains: "I've never seen a survey where people state they buy air transportation by the colour of the airplanes." In fact, Southwest stands apart with colour schemes that in no way can be mistaken for other, more traditional, corporate airlines. Southwest also makes unabashed use of the word "love". Love permeates everything Southwest does. The company is headquartered at Love Field in Dallas. They use a heart in their logo. And they passionately put employees first. Southwest is even listed on the New York Stock exchange as "LUV." Naturally, the External Brand spreads this message with ad campaigns such as "How Do We Love You?" which featured the entire flight schedule. Another, titled "We're Spreading Love" advertised the rapid growth of the airline.

External Brand is focused entirely on customers and communities that will be attracted by your business model (Products & Services) as well as the message, visuals, sounds, shapes and other branding signals that vividly describe enhance and reinforce your brand promise. External Brand reveals itself in physical, tangible forms. Think of everything from websites to washrooms; customer greetings to TV commercials; sales kits to store décor. Consistency in the use of words, pictures, colours, shapes and sounds, carefully weaving together relevant messages speaking to the customer in the language of the customer.

Nothing happens in a business until a customer decides to buy something. And the decision to buy doesn't occur unless there has been a positive sensory impact. Typically, people make buying decisions based on what they feel and then justify their purchase logically, afterwards. Powerful External Brands like Southwest reflect a compelling combination of positioning, packaging and promotion that grabs attention, generates emotion, and sparks action.

INTERNAL BRAND: Embracing the Promise

Great marketing starts from the inside out.

It doesn't take a frequent flier long to notice that the "culture" at Southwest is very different from many of its more business-oriented competitors. Southwest has staked its brand strategy on a fun, light-hearted and irreverent culture with an upbeat staff. One of the major hiring criteria is how often an applicant smiles during his or her interview. Southwest feels it can train anyone to do the job, but it can't teach a person to have a positive attitude.

Internal Brand focuses on how people join, come together and form what emerges as the Company Character. This Character will be shaped by the levels of collaboration, conversation and adherence to codes of conduct, eventually becoming a Tribal Community that embraces its own and those it attracts.

A company is its people. Products and services can't be manufactured, delivered, advertised, or sold without the people who make up a company. Lack of a well-defined Internal Brand is often what creates disconnects - both internally and externally. Do your employees believe 1001% in what your brand stands for? The products and services you offer? Have you created a climate where people with different skill sets, backgrounds, personalities and talents can mesh together and move in one direction?

A vibrant Internal Brand accelerates levels of employee buy-in, operational efficiencies and opportunities to enhance the brand through each point of customer contact. More than window dressing, there is a hard business case to be made for any organization that can develop higher levels of discretionary effort from its people. There is considerable research supporting this conclusion: High-morale companies like Southwest are faster and more profitable than miserable slowpokes. Southwest enhances this advantage by jumping into the blogosphere with a platform for customers and employees to communicate with one another. Southwest is fully aware that, on average, each passenger has about ten contacts, every time he flies. Do the math. Through the call centre, website, at the check-in and on-board the plane, any airline that moves 10 million passengers per year, benefits from an energized vibrant Internal Brand capitalizing on those 100 million interactions.

INDIVIDUAL BRAND: Believing the Promise
Talent-fit. Shared values. Belief.

These are three essential qualities for anyone wanting to join a Seamless Brand™. Skills and qualifications are not enough to make a good match. Individuals need to believe in what the brand stands for or it's no dice. And the onus is on the individual to embrace what the Internal Brand is all about. In other words, the tail never wags the dog.

"Seamless" companies like Southwest treat its people with dignity as opposed to disposable commodities. The lack of lay-offs and strikes at Southwest Airlines means employees feel secure in their jobs, enjoying high levels of compensation and benefits.

In a Seamless Brand™, individuals are attracted by the opportunity to express their unique gifts within the structure of a company and the customers they serve. These individuals recognize it is their responsibility to develop their capacity to contribute to the Tribal Community that serves as a canvas to express those talents. People who "bleed the brand" won't surf Monster.com looking for new opportunities. They won't badmouth the business to friends or family at cocktail parties or backyard barbecues. Individuals who truly believe in their brand reveal it in everyday actions, seamlessly living the promise; acting as ambassadors while looking for new ways to improve delivery.

However, developing a Seamless Brand™ is impossible unless the individuals who join possess an emotional connection to the type of work that they do. They have discovered a greater meaning or purpose in tasks that need performing to get the job done. Those who just "do it for the money" eventually wither and rust. Only those who value shared abundance over a scarcity mentality need apply. In other words, the interests of the greater good rank above those of one's self.

EXECUTIVE BRAND: Inspiring & Living the Promise

Legend has it that Herb Kelleher and one of his law clients, Texas businessman Rollin King, created the Southwest concept on a cocktail napkin in a San Antonio restaurant. Rather than the traditional hub-and-spoke method, King drew a triangle on the napkin symbolizing the Dallas, Houston and San Antonio as the routes. Kelleher who became Executive Chairman in 1978 is one of the few men in America who still smokes and drinks without apology. Years ago, when he turned over the reins as chief executive, Kelleher sat in a Frank Sinatra-like pose for the cover of *Fortune*. A glass of Wild Turkey in one hand. A cigarette in the other. Over the years, whenever reporters would ask him the secret to Southwest's success, Kelleher had a stock response. "You have to treat your employees like customers," he told *Fortune* in 2001. "When you treat them right, then they will treat your outside customers right. That has been a powerful competitive weapon for us."

Brand strength is always determined by a single word.

Trust.

And trust only develops through the way a person or a company acts on what they have promised. Nowhere is this more critical at the executive level as a cynical world insists on more integrity in business. Ironically, Integrity and Integration have the same Latin root integritas, which means "honesty, completeness, soundness". Over time, it becomes a form of currency for brands like Southwest and CEO's like Kelleher who made a hefty deposit in that account when he explained, "We've never had layoffs, we could have made more money if we furloughed people. But we don't do that. And we honour them constantly. Our people know that if they are sick, we will take care of them. If there are occasions or grief or joy, we will be there with them. They know that we value them as people, not just cogs in a machine."

Like any living organism, a Seamless Brand™ is committed to growth - and the many forms growth takes. Size and bottom-line results are not the only ways to measure growth. Other factors could include intellectual, creative, or personal, but it's essential some form of growth take place. Otherwise, the alternatives are stagnation, decay, and eventually, collapse. That's true for a company - and equally true for a career.

Only trustworthy, growth-oriented executives can effectively inspire a compelling story with clarity that reflects the company's vision. With clarity - a mental image held in one's thoughts - the brand has an opportunity to occupy top shelf space in the minds of internal and external customers, and leverage its full value.

Trust. Growth. Clarity.

Leaders who miss these crucial aspects of brand building - because of the cost, time, or energy required - will likely pay a much higher price than those who don't. Ultimately, the role of CEO evolves into one of Chief Engagement Officer, which requires a fundamental shift from seeing the business world being made up of products and services, to seeing environments made up of relationships. It's a mental shift - one that requires leaders to focus less on the "doing" of leading and more on the "being" of serving.

It's easier said than done. The human mind craves a mental model of a static structured world with rigid boundaries - as opposed to visualizing open, vibrant, interconnected human ecosystems. That being said, the Seamless Brand™ framework can serve as a way for anyone in an organization to make sense of an increasingly chaotic business world.

Inspired by Kelleher and his successors, Southwest has enjoyed more than three decades of stunning clarity on their brand and business model:

1. Identify customers we want to serve.
2. Be the low cost provider.

The first item caters to luring customers thinking about driving or taking the bus. Southwest offers short-haul flights, priced in such a way it may be preferable to fly than drive. The second entails frequent but no-frills service, with no food being served and flying only one model of airplane to save on efficiencies. From its birth in 1971 — Southwest has succeeded by daring to be different: offering low fares to its passengers by eliminating unnecessary services, providing their own wacky brand of in-flight entertainment from its employees and using a remarkable hedge strategy to save hundreds of millions of dollars in fuel costs. For most airlines, fuel constitutes about 40% of their costs, up from 10 percent just a few years ago. But not Southwest. Not when 70 percent of the company's fuel is hedged at $51 a barrel — which is fantastic when your competitors are paying the going rate as world oil prices climb to about $126 a barrel. Can you see why investors who bought $1,000 worth of Southwest stock at the IPO in 1972, would own investments worth about $1.8 million today?

Product or price advantages are difficult to come by in any category, because they can be easily duplicated. Creating a strong customer service culture, however, is easier said than done. Calgary-based WestJet has been able to duplicate the Southwest model and pull it off in Canada - and yes, it has led to incredible market share growth and profitability.

But, as the WestJet "Rock Star of People" Tyson Matheson of the HR department once shared, "It has been anything but easy, but if it was, everybody else would be doing it."

Few brands have figured out how to do it - align Marketing, HR and Operations with both speed and passion – in the same manner a small, Texas-based airline began showing WestJet and the rest of the world in the early 1970's.

How many miles must a brand walk down, before they call it seamless?

The answer, my friend, is blowin' in a wind from Southwest.

"A company is stronger if it is bound by love rather than by fear"

-HERB KELLEHER

10
Wheels on the Bus

Legendary management guru Peter Drucker argues "At most, one-third of hiring decisions turn out right; one-third are minimally effective; and one-third are outright failures." Drucker adds, "In no other area of management would we put up with such miserable performance. When you stop and think about it, Peter's got a point. But does that mean most companies have about a .300 batting average when it comes to selecting talent? Those may be Hall of Fame statistics in baseball but most business owners I know wouldn't be giving each other high-fives for swinging and missing 7 out of 10 times.

In his landmark work, Good to Great, Jim Collins studied more than 6,000 companies over a 15-year period, and concluded that great companies become so by making sure "you get the right people on the bus and sitting in the right seats while getting the wrong ones off". Most business execs get that concept, but then what? In other words, how does one pull that off?

Good question. One demanding a great answer.

For the sake of simplicity, stick with the bus as a metaphor for your business model. Think of the outside of the vehicle as your external brand, representing everything in a tangible form that would make customers and future employees decide to hop on. So what is it about your bus that makes it stand apart from all the other vehicles in your category?

The engine represents the actual business model (how you make money) so that the bus is able to move forward.

The route you follow and the destination you hope to reach is your vision. It's not enough to know where you want to go. Have you figured out why you want to make the trip in the first place?

Assuming you have a bus worthy of getting the right people

in the first place, (not "two feet and a heartbeat"), start thinking of recruitment and hiring as the "wheels" of your bus.

As they turn smoothly, so does your business and your brand.

Any road worthy talent acquisition strategy will include the look, feel and essence of your bus and whether you have the horsepower and a well-conceived plan to reach your destination.

The more you attract a better quality of people to your bus in the first place, the better your hiring decisions will be. So, what shape is your bus in? Is it capable of transporting great talent? Have you built a sleek, comfortable coach, equipped to enjoy breath-taking views of Canada's panoramic Rocky Mountains or does it resemble a beat-up and rusted iron lung, trapped in the snarl and exhaust of the urban jungle?

Where do you believe the line-up of eager applicants will form?

As if the challenges posed by an aging workforce aren't enough, the pendulum shift created by today's plugged-in, wired-and-wiser, 25-and-under crowd is demanding something more from your bus. They'll want to know (and will quickly find out) what's under the hood. And they'll text their friends about it.

You already know high turnover rates are bad for business. Financially expensive. Emotionally draining. Experience has shown that in the past when you've made a bad hiring decision, it was impossible to fix through training, coaching or leadership.

You won't bat .1000, but there are many other ways to boost your talent acquisition average. Much will depend on the number and quality of filters you deploy before someone jumps on board. It starts with having an accurate picture of your company's persona; what your bus is all about in terms of what it stands for and against; the intangible elements of its character that are key to any business journey. If a candidate doesn't fit that character or culture – it's already game over.

Don't issue the ticket.

Regrettably, far too many companies miss the opportunity to allow talent to self-select by masking their culture with cliché-ridden, corporate-speak job ads that do nothing to let an outsider look in. Consider the following:

Do you believe for a minute that real talent actually buys that chest-thumping generic crap anymore?

Now consider an alternative, persona-based approach that speaks less about the company and more directly to the type of candidate you hope will be intrigued by who you are and what your brand is all about.

Shouldn't you spend your career-peak years in a job so amazing you'll want to stay until you retire?

Executive Director / CEO Doggie Heaven

Doggie Heaven, a nationally recognized centre for abused and neglected dogs, has all the building blocks in place to greatly expand our ability to provide service to our community. We are seeking a CEO to stack those blocks into a powerful, leading-edge organization, and to then nurture it as it thrives.

What We Are Looking For:
- Someone who is just as comfortable rolling on the floor with a pile of Labradors and Shepherds as they are networking in an Armani tux or Versace gown with corporate leaders;
- An effective and passionate writer and speaker, comfortable in the role of public figure;
- A leader and mentor with an inclusive style, whose former employees want to keep in touch;

The first carbon copy ad talks about the job. The second speaks to a specific customer in the language of the customer.

Looking at the choice of wording and tones of these ads, which bus do you think will attract and board the right candidates?

Never lose sight of the fact that before applications start rolling in, your brand first needs to be noticed and then considered.

Other great ways to share your culture and get noticed by prospective employees is through written or video descriptions on your website. Check out the mojo of British technology firm Media Snackers who aren't afraid to share what they're all about at www.mediasnackers.com. Imagine how someone interested in a career in social media marketing would feel after getting to know these ubercool cats a little bit better. Some examples from the "Manifesto" section of their website:

MEDIASNACKERS

Everything we do must be kick ass—the overarching MediaSnackers mantra.

Be fluid—(reflect the market and) bend, change, divert, redefine, fluxuate, react, stretch, evolve, reinvent, be dynamic and stay organic.

Leading is a choice—not a position.

Play constantly—with words, ideas, technology, platforms, structures and others. It's the best way to learn.

Real life has more bandwidth—faces are better than Facebook, getting out there, making people 3D and pressing palms still rules!

Believe in values—they are assets not to be sold. Meaning, we scrutinize every potential client and are selective who we work with (no tobacco companies or fast-food chains please).

Experience doesn't matter—not when you're trying new stuff. That's why it's called new. The success is nearly always in the attempt.

Make it personal—yes, MediaSnackers is a business but we're people first.

Collaborate—Albert Einstein said it best: "Nothing great was ever done alone." We like company.

Conversation over advertising—no direct mail-outs or fliers. We haven't the time or belief in interruption marketing. We ensure we kick ass and promote this. More signal, less noise, or, simple stories, well told.

Any Questions?

Once your employer brand gets noticed and candidates are lining up, more filters can be added to the process, including telephone screening, reference checks, group and peer interviews, writing exercises, "American Idol" type auditions, orientation "training camps", as well as a judicious use of psychometric assessment instruments.

With an increasing number of candidates demonstrating polished interviewee skills, why not consider replacing the balding tires of the traditional hire-at-a-glance method.

Research from Michigan State University reveals hiring decisions based on "gut feel" from a single face-to-face interview offers only a 14% chance of being successful. Even if solely going with your "gut" does work out, chances are nothing has been done to structure and duplicate this process. There is no way to determine patterns for what works and what doesn't. And it depends heavily on the skill of the interviewer.

Adding specific, scripted steps to your hiring process tilts the odds in your favour. For example, the same MSU study discovered that whenever reference and background checks are added to the mix, success ratios increase to 26%. When job-fit assessments are added, the ratio jumps to 76%. Ultimately, any hiring decision will come down to a "gut" decision - but a systemized funnel that attracts candidates who share similar values, coupled with well-designed filters can add a wealth of objective data to an otherwise hit-and-miss process.

Your company's "flex appeal" will always equal the level of talent on your bus. So what are you strategically doing to assess talent? Is your brand in tip-top shape to the point where it attracts the right people to begin with? Common sense tells us that if a person doesn't have an underlying talent for something, they will always struggle. That being the case, are you doing everything possible (for both the candidate and your company) to ensure a proper fit?

Finding and keeping top notch talent will always be an issue unless you know who you are and what you want from your talent in the first place. That's tough without a compelling brand, designed to separate contenders from pretenders before deciding on who suits up as full-time players.

Is it time to do some heavy lifting and grease your "talent acquisition wheels"?

"When I meet successful people I ask 100 questions as to what they attribute their success to. It is usually the same: persistence, hard work and hiring good people."

-KIANA TOM

11
From a Wrench to a Wiki

One day (maybe, you've had one of those days) Pierre decided enough was enough. Fifty-plus hours a week with his head stuck underneath someone else's hood was getting to be more than he could stomach. The work itself wasn't the problem. Brake jobs, ball joints, rack and pinion, carburetors, transmissions were a breeze. But life as a 25-year old mechanic was starting to mean very little if it meant working his guts out to build someone else's dream and not his own.

Six months after Pierre started swinging a wrench at Ralph's Auto Repair, he let the boss know that someday he would like to own a piece of the business. Maybe take it over one day. And Ralph, thoroughly impressed with the energy and enthusiasm of his best employee – responded by saying "You keep sticking this out, and within five years, maybe eight, the whole thing could be yours".

Five years later, Pierre decided to follow up with his boss on that promise.

"Well to tell you the truth, Pierre, I can't see that happening for another five years or so, maybe eight".

To himself, Pierre muttered "It'll be more like a dozen. Likely never".

Deep down, he knew the only answer that made sense.

It was time to trade in his wrench. But for what?

At that moment, Pierre decided to follow what his "gut" was saying when it came to owning a business. The same instincts that served him well when, as a youngster, he purchased a box of unwanted Olympic souvenir pins for 20 bucks and sold them for a profit of about $500 at a local flea market. A return on investment of about 2500% generated by an 8-year old who still liked to watch the occasional episode of Sesame Street.

Growing up, Pierre had been intrigued by the world of real estate. He admired his Dad, who owned several rental properties, always generating positive cash flow while paying down mortgages. In fact, Pierre had followed in Victor's footsteps, buying his first rental property at the age of 19.

He started wondering and dreaming.

"Maybe I could turn this hobby into a full-time business and become a contractor specializing in new home construction. But find a way to do it differently. Not like all the others".

So, Martell Home Builders was about to be launched as a full-time venture with little more than high hopes and a gut feeling. But first there was some unfinished business that needed taking care of.

When Pierre walked through the service bay and turned in his overalls and letter of resignation, Ralph was floored. And once the deer in the headlights look faded, the boss looked his favourite employee square in the eye and with great sincerity told him, *"You are truly, truly, truly making a big mistake. The biggest mistake of your life. You don't know what you're getting into, owning a business. It's a lot harder than it looks."*

Austrian economist Joseph Schumpeter, who escaped the Nazis and taught at Harvard, defined an entrepreneur as a person who is willing and able to drive "creative destruction" across markets and industries. Simply put, it means the process by which old ways of doing things are replaced by new ways. One of Schumpeter's students, management guru and fellow Austrian, Peter Drucker stated that you can boil entrepreneurship down to one word - risk. The amount of willingness one has to put his or her career and financial security on the line for the sake of an idea. In Pierre's first couple of months in business, he teetered on the edge of destruction, discovering first-hand what no dictionary definition or PhD could teach him about risk.

"With two foundations in the ground, three people on payroll and suppliers bills piling up, I am literally robbing Pierre to pay

Paul. Maxed out four credit cards, re-mortgaged my house. I'm stressed to the max, losing sleep, flirting with bankruptcy and starting to think maybe Ralph was right. I honestly thought these homes would just somehow sell on their own, and since they didn't, I am learning some tough lessons and learning them fast".

With the sheriff less than a week away, Pierre managed to keep the company alive by convincing younger brother, Moe to buy one of his first units. He made a decision to sacrifice all potential profit in the deal, securing enough cash to keep the wolves at bay and buy a few more weeks.

Pierre used his time well.

Hit the fast-forward button.

Less than 12 months later, Martell Home Builders emerged as one of Canada's most innovative home-building companies.

There are few that can compare to the "Martell Experience".

Pierre's brainchild features a web-enabled platform that drives a seamless, start-to-finish project management system, complete with timeline and fully interactive client log-in software. New home construction is guaranteed in four months or less with the "99-Day Construction Countdown". Employing creative guerrilla marketing tactics and using FaceBook, Twitter and other social media applications, Martell Home Builders has generated more than 80% of its sales privately, adding to its bottom-line by avoiding MLS commissions. They also turned heads at their first-ever trade show where Pierre's booth was the only one recording live TV-type interviews with local celebrities and other exhibitors. Not only did more people stop by for a look but all of the interviews were posted on YouTube with the viral effect pushing the Martell Home Builders website on the front page of the Google rankings within ten days.

Clearly, Pierre is doing everything he can to turn an otherwise traditional industry on its ear. And then kick it in the ass. Some of the cool stuff woven in to the "Martell Experience" includes:

The Client Log-in - A simple, web-based application that allows the customer, vendors and the MHB team to stay in the loop in terms of decisions, options, timelines, status. An on-line hub detailing the entire project - everything from building permits to architectural drawings and "Don't Forget" lists.

Wireless Video - Since Pierre can't drive around to all job sites and see if sub-contractors have shown up, he simply logs on and accesses a live camera that monitors each job site. He can look in real time and see what's really going.

Wiki Operations Manual – What got you here won't keep you here. Pierre understands business processes are in a constant state of change - so they need to be fluid. The day of printed off materials have disappeared like the dinosaur and this allows team members to design and implement systems that need to be in place, allowing MHB to keep their brand promise. For example, one of the project managers, upon hearing customer feedback on going a week without a phone after moving, was able to develop a "Top Ten List of Things to Think About Before You Move" and post it in the Wiki so everyone would automatically provide it as part of the New Customer Orientation process.

iPhones - Every MHB employee has one. Preloaded with a 3-minute Martell Home Builder video posted on You Tube that shares the company's "story". The iPhone is also connected to all web applications, so when a client asks, "How is my house coming along?" any employee can access the latest on-line photos that monitor progress on a weekly-basis.

You Tube Videos - In an effort to better connect with key stakeholders, suppliers, partners, and others, Pierre will deliver a message on video, post it on You Tube, and e-mail links to those he wants to reach.

Geo-Tagged Photos - Photos that monitor construction progress are geo-tagged with an MHB watermark. Newer cameras equipped with built-in GPS technology have the ability to drive search engine hits. Anyone searching on-line for photos in the Moncton area automatically discover branded, MHB pictures.

There are also Twitter updates, Delicious bookmarks, a blog and other technologies to keep a growing legion of construction fans seamlessly linked to everything Pierre is doing and thinking about.

And the entire business model is now ready for duplication in markets across the country. The real-time operations manual, that utilizes wiki technology to stay ahead of the curve, epitomizes Pierre's strategy to deal with a rapidly changing world and industry. Essentially, Martell Home Builders is a company that embraces the new Theory of Wikinomics - and its principles of Openness, Peering, Sharing and Acting Globally. It's a model that allows both customers and business partners to plug into the brand – while the rest of the world watches with growing admiration.

Pierre's story has gone viral to the point where influential bloggers such as Jason Falls of Louisville, KY raved about what he has created with a compelling endorsement in the fall of 2008 at www.socialmediaexplorer.com. In Jason's words, *"I've never had a house built but have heard horror stories of projects being tens of thousands of dollars over budget, months and months behind schedule and problem after problem with the contractor, permits and more. What defines Martell's unique selling proposition is transparency. You're going to know where he is at all times. You're going to know what's going on with your house at all times. Advertising, customer relations, vendor relations, public relations, website execution, social media and more are all by-products of the umbrella strategic approach to give the customer a home building and buying experience like no other. Whether intentional or not, Martell went through the strategic process of defining their audience, establishing their objectives, developing strategies to accomplish those objectives with the audience and then - after all that was established - decide the tools (on- and off-line) or mechanisms to execute the strategy"*. Accolades such as these are what made the Greater Moncton Chamber of Commerce sit up and take notice in October of 2008, as MHB captured top marketing honours at the annual Business Excellence Awards – less than two years after start-up.

Some people ask, "How does he do it?"

How does an otherwise normal guy out of a garage connect the desire for innovation to the persistence required to get the job gets done?

According to Pierre, any formula for entrepreneurial success can be boiled down to a single phrase; "Be willing to do whatever most people aren't. There is a reason why only 5% of any population base controls about 95% of the money and that's because those are the kind of people who will do all of the little pain-in-the-ass things that most people can't be bothered doing."

With the help of a web-savvy entrepreneurial older brother and other business mentors, Pierre also learned quickly to "stop trading time for money". As he explains, "The key to business growth is leverage, leverage, leverage and you only learn that by surrounding yourself with other people who think that way and can teach you. My brother knew nothing about contracting per se, but he knew a ton of stuff about leverage, so each time something would come up about our business model, he would challenge existing assumptions and call bullshit. That's one of the great things about learning from my brother and all of the books, seminars and people he and others in my circle have introduced me to. Once you learn not to accept status quo on anything - and figure out how to stop trading time for money, the sky is the limit."

Perhaps, Pierre's "can do" characteristics are best captured in this fashion; brought you today by the "Number 4" and the "Letter I":

1. **Imagination** – Ability to sense early stages of opportunity.
2. **Inspiration** – Believing in and selling yourself that you can do it.
3. **Initiative** – Taking action - doing what others aren't willing to do.
4. **Implementation** – Systems designed to create and keep customers.

It's tempting to want to trade your "wrench for a wiki" and make the shift from employee to entrepreneur. However, any decision to do so requires a mindset to be willing to do what most people would never dream of doing. Many who claim they want to own a business are really saying they want to own an *already successful* business. How many people do you know that possess the intestinal fortitude to roll the dice in the first place, are willing to do the thousands of hours of lonely, heavy lifting, and endure the sweaty palms and sleepless nights at "gut check" time?

One day, you may decide enough is enough and start

giving considerable thought to building your own dream. Trade your wrench for a wiki. Or, perhaps you decide to get serious about finding ways to lift your existing business to entirely new levels.

But here are some questions that need mulling over.

- Do you have the inner strength to trust your instincts and emotions, even in the absence of explicit knowledge and information?

- Are you internally motivated to the point where you would be ready to sacrifice it all for the sake of an idea? In other words, how many loose screws do you have to go with the nuts and bolts of your business model?

- How willing are you to work, sweat, screw-up, learn and find creative solutions that exist in new technologies; become remarkable in your own way and knock competitors on their keesters?

Not too long ago, Pierre brought his truck back to Ralph's shop for a tune-up. This time, the former boss took him aside, looked him in the eye and again with great sincerity, said, *"Pierre, I'm really proud of you."*

Someday, when Pierre is making millions and relaxing on a yacht somewhere in the Caribbean, people will say "Boy did he get lucky with that contracting business. Guess that kid was just in the right place at the right time."

In the end, Ralph was right.

Going from a wrench to a wiki – and doing it in less than a year - is a lot harder than it looks.

"Capitalism demands the best of every man and rewards him accordingly. It leaves every man free to go as far as his ability and ambition will carry him"
-AYN RAND

12
Brand Runner

"I had no idea I would run into so many interesting people"

Bobbi Jo is new in town.

And after hearing what a friend had to say over cocktails one evening, she is intrigued by the idea of indulging her running habit while expanding her social network. Acting on word-of-mouth advertising, Bobbi Jo shows up on a sunny Sunday morning to join over 100 other Running Room fans for the weekly practice run. Upwardly mobile professionals and bureaucrats mix easily with soccer moms and seniors as a shared identity emerges - linked by the lure of getting fit in the great outdoors.

Bobbi Jo likes what she sees.

She will definitely be back.

This story repeats itself thousands of times each week, allowing The Running Room to stand alone as a "category of one" with a chain of 92 corporately-owned stores in Canada and the U.S. Building a brand identity around the needs of a niche customer allows The Running Room to overcome a challenge facing every independent retailer today: "How do I compete against the big guys?"

Would you believe it's oh so simple?

Astonishingly simple.

Just pick something. Do it better than anyone else. Turn niche customers into raving fans. And provide an environment that allows those fans to form common bonds that morph into a cult-like community.

The Running Room makes this happen by knowing who they are and what they stand for, an essence that originates with company founder John Stanton. *"The one race we all face is against aging,"* says Stanton. *"We've been able to introduce people to exercise in a gentler way. We're different, however, because we are specialists. We only do running".*

That's it folks.

They only do running.

The Running Room's focus, commitment and brand promise was forged in 1981, when an out-of-shape, overweight Stanton went on a 3-kilometre run with his young sons that made him realize he had to change his lifestyle. In fact, Stanton would secretly run before dawn because he felt self-conscious about having his neighbours see *"this chubby little guy"* who could only run from lamppost to lamppost before having to slow down and walk to catch his breath. *"I thought this guy peeping through his drapes in the morning - I called him "Curtain Charlie" — was laughing at me. Like most people when they first start running, I was self-conscious. Then one day he knocked on my door and said, 'John, I really admire you. I've been watching you lose weight and quit smoking. Can you show me how you did it?'"*

As Stanton dropped 60 pounds in three months and began racing, he discovered practical advice for the novice runner was hard to find. Stanton recalls being frustrated with a teenage salesperson at a major chain store. *"He was trying to sell me a pair of racing flats when I needed training shoes. He didn't understand the difference."* Stanton sensed a market niche, and The Running Room was born. Alongside the gear and footwear, The Running Room sells a lifestyle of wellness, offering running clinics and practice runs for everyone from the beginner to the marathoner-in-training. *"If you are knowledgeable about your sport, you can probably go to a big box store and come away satisfied. But if you're new to the sport or trying to improve, you're not going to go there."*

And since people talk, and others like Bobbi Jo listen, most newcomers discover this difference through their natural networks.

Rather than blast hot air through the airwaves or chew up the forest with newspaper advertising, The Running Room relies on the organic power of word-of-mouth; offering free, no-strings-attached, biweekly practice runs that depart from each store Wednesdays at 6 p.m. and Sunday mornings at 8:30 a.m. Runners like Bobbi Jo eventually form tight bonds with other like-minded folks as the strategy draws in customers, while providing a social context that makes it fun to run. And then she tells one person and so on. And so on. More than 80% of this roving pack of acolytes will wind up buying, wearing and using Running Room products and services. Just being fitted with the proper footwear is an experience in itself. Staff will spend an hour or more analyzing your running pattern, stride, gait, etc., to ensure a proper fit.

As John explained earlier, it's simple.

They only do running.

Since the first store opened in 1984, The Running Room's revenue has grown an average of 27% per year and has established a beachhead in the U.S. by opening a cluster of stores in Minnesota. They are a textbook example for any company looking to turn customers into converts: harnessing modern technology to help deliver old-fashioned, hold-your-hand guidance that soaks the skeptics and washes the wallflowers with a can-do attitude and a feeling of being "in the club". The company has been profitable every year since it opened and while average retailers turn inventory over fewer than three times a year, The Running Room's average is closer to four. Annual revenues have reached the $100 million range and the company employs roughly 900 people. Despite the lofty numbers, The Running Room remains a family-owned business with a folksy corporate culture that values fun, fitness and community giving, over mega-growth at any price.

John Stanton is also a best-selling author of four books and was once named to MacLean's Magazine Honour Roll as one of ten Canadians making a difference in our nation for his contribution to health through fitness. He manages to run at least two or three marathons a year, with plenty of half-marathons to go with his 40 to 60 kilometre weekly pace, and a work schedule that sees him on the road about 300 days a year. Says he's like the "A&W Root Bear" of the company. John is well aware of the implications of the phrase "workaholic" but points out, *True success is never knowing if you're working or playing. If it's going to a road race, talking to runners, customers, or just going for a run or a walk, are all just fun for me. I think true success is making sure work is play."*

Meanwhile, later that same day, while sipping on a latte at Starbucks, Bobbi Jo is raving about her Running Room experience when Darren and Courtney can't help but overhear. A conversation ensues as the newcomers join in to share what they have gained from their involvement. Several people wind up chatting for well over 20 minutes about running do's and don'ts, road trips to PEI, New York, Saint John and Vancouver, and people they have met along the way. All the while, The Running Room brand continues to secure a share of customers minds - with little, if any, traditional advertising.

In effect, The Running Room has created a cult brand in much the same fashion as Harley-Davidson, Oprah and Apple - those who dare to be different knowing they're not just selling a product or service. And while cult brands seem exclusive, they're actually inclusive, going out of their way to make potential converts feel welcome. From a business owner's perspective, they are also recession-resistant. Famed novelist Thomas Wolfe once referred to a cult as a religion with no political power. In the world of free enterprise, customers vote with their pocketbooks. The only brands that get elected are those that prove themselves worthy through the value of the experience.

What is your business doing to inspire brand loyalty?

Forget about your product or service for a moment. How does your brand connect with your customers' emotional needs? Is there a single thing you could laser-focus on and do sooo much better than anyone else?

Figuring out whether you've got a potential cult brand on your hands isn't going to happen overnight - or by itself.

Start watching. Observe intently. Listen to what is being communicated in everyday conversations.

Really listen.

See if you can make connections between the surface of idle chit-chat and a potential business model that lies underneath. Can you think of a better time to get out of the office and run to put on your imaginary branding shoes?

What is that one thing your business could do that would leave every lazy-ass, couch potato competitor gasping for air?

And choking on the dust from your trail.

"Out of the silver heat mirage he ran. The sky burned, and under him the paving was a black mirror reflecting sun-fire. Sweat sprayed his skin with each foot strike so that he ran in a hot mist of his own creation. With each slap on the softened asphalt, his soles absorbed heat that rose through his arches and ankles and the stems of his shins. It was a carnival of pain, but he loved each stride because running distilled him to his essence and the heat hastened this distillation."

- JAMES TABOR, from "The Runner"

13
A Phone Call to Phil

"What you're talking about is a business case for love."

Those were the words Phil uttered from four time zones away, while digesting key elements of **The Seamless Brand™**.

Phil continued, *"The two greatest forces on this planet are love and fear. People are constantly seeking comfort, ways to stay safe - and from what I can tell - most of us want to honour the womb in some way and remain attached to what is comfortable. What you're talking about here is a way to reduce or even remove unnecessary and untimely unproductive and unprofitable fear from a company. It's brilliant!"*

Phil knows the price of fear more than most.

For more than three decades, he has been working with teams and individuals to optimize performance. Now in his mid-sixties, Phil gained international notoriety while working with one small group of business owners, caught at a crossroads. The partners were struggling with strategic direction - whether to add a new member to the executive team or perhaps, just pack it in and call it a day. It didn't help that this volatile, dysfunctional group was also plagued by substance abuse issues, unresolved conflicts, and inner demons.

There was a lot at stake.

These three executives represent a business that annually racks up revenues in the hundreds of millions of dollars. A lot of people depend on this brand for their livelihood. For legions of others, it feeds and nourishes their very souls. A brand known worldwide to millions and Phil has been assigned the job of trying to hold it all together.

But wait, that's not all.

Phil's consulting sessions were to be recorded in full view, in front of a Hollywood film crew. With the mask of multi-millionaire egos removed under glaring lights, while ducking the harsh sounds of F-bombs and slamming doors. But, over a two-and-half year period, Phil Towle helped put a psychologically broken, Humpty Dumpty version of Metallica back on the heavy metal wall, reviving the legendary band's career and earning a reputation for himself as a leading authority on dysfunctions that plague any group endeavour.

Metallica: Some Kind of Monster depicts the human condition at its rawest and purest, simultaneously repairing old wounds and preventing new ones. Pared down from 1600 hours of footage, the movie goes beyond being just a documentary about a heavy metal band, and forces us to examine the lurking thought monsters in our own heads. Monsters that affect our everyday interactions, communication, and relationships.

Looking back on his time with Metallica, Towle reflects, *"I see the Lars/James relationship as a love story. I saw it when I first met with them. When I was doing psychotherapy I saw it with couples. Basically they needed to be respected and loved and they needed to exercise that love like all couples do. When issues aren't dealt with, love gets replaced by resentment and negativity. When James wrote "Enter Sandman," he courageously invited the alienated of our society and in each of us to openly express our fears and insecurities and alienation. He captured the hearts and souls of that part of us that wasn't able to talk about our hurt or had trouble expressing that. When people can come out and talk about the secrets of their pain, that's a love story.*

Drummer Lars Ulrich has been quoted as saying, *"Phil helped saved the band. But it was also our willingness to go there. It was the right combination of people ready to explore this stuff - not just for the survival of the band, but for our own sanity."* From the perspective of front man James Hetfield, *"People know us as crazy rock idols; but this film is the broken down, really just struggling, humans. Somewhere, in the middle, it is really just us... It's good to check in with each other and we had never done that before."*

It was costly work - Towle's fee was a whopping $40,000 a month - but it got results. "St. Anger," Metallica's first album in five years, went platinum and earned a Grammy, and the band received MTV's highest honour, the Icon Award.

Given his accomplishments and the role he played in resurrecting an act that has sold over 100 million records, it seemed fitting to invite Towle to weigh in with an opinion on the TSB framework. The California-based career coach responded this way: *"In any dysfunctional family there are three unspoken rules: don't talk, don't trust, and don't feel. In order to survive on the road in a rock band or inside a company those unspoken rules unwittingly come into play. You can never admit you're tired or hurting. What you're saying is that the traditional, top-down pyramid model called an org chart unwittingly conspires to create dysfunction and fear in companies without anyone ever being aware of it. That's interesting. Looking at the Seamless Brand structure from a horizontal perspective, one that flows from an intangible core, would allow everyone connected with the organization to plug into its true energy source. That's my take on it."*

Thanks for the feedback Phil.

Author Patrick Lencioni may well have been writing about Towle and Metallica in his best-selling book, The Five Dysfunctions of a Team. According to Lencioni in his fable about a fictitious Silicon Valley firm, the first dysfunction is Absence of Trust. It's the one that most hinders a team from being effective. The fear of being vulnerable with team members prevents trust from being built, eventually leading to fear of conflict, lack of commitment, avoidance of accountability and inattention to results. Sad, but oh so true.

The primary role of a leader is to be the first one to be vulnerable, and create an environment where it's safe to be vulnerable. Sometimes, bringing a neutral third party to the table permits enough trust to emerge so that healthy conflict and debate become possible. Teams unable to engage in healthy conflict become a collection of masterful puppets subjected to an invisible king called Artificial Harmony. Before long, the sandman enters your company in the form of mask-wearing, two-faced "yes men". Any shred of company spirit slowly fades to black.

A rock band is just like the inside of any company or family, dysfunctional as any other and when calibration is off, people predictably attack each other. In the case of Metallica, James lost his only parent at 16 and felt abandoned. Lars came from a comfortable background, but needed control. Guitarist Kirk Hammett grew up as the mediator in his family. They carried their childhood roles into their adult lives. Towle points out the roles we develop as teenagers don't work forever and that's why many can relate to the human struggle and transformation captured in *"Some Kind of Monster"*.

Great athletes, artists, academics - and in particular business leaders - all want to push themselves beyond their limits. Be it faster, riskier or more outrageous – the goal is to see how far they can take their craft to find out what they're made of.

It is in that moment they come face to face with love. The highest form of energy. In fact, the source of energy in any business is love. It's why it began in the first place.

Logic would dictate that if brands are about feelings and not facts, and if the two polarities of energy create the emotions of Love and Fear, one can conclude that that which is not Love, is Fear.

Hetfield, Ulrich and Hammet formed Metallica out of nothing. And they couldn't have done it without love. Their songs all express pain about unrequited love; however, many adults get scared by this kind of music simply because they don't understand it.

Likewise, many business leaders feel apprehensive and start to squirm whenever the subject of love needs to be dealt with. But when you stop and reflect on this, does anything else matter?

Is your organization based on any of these truths?

Do you know many companies or executive teams that would be willing to face fear and appear vulnerable the way Metallica did? In full view of millions of fans they knew would be watching? Never knowing for certain over the course of nearly three uncertain years how the movie would end?

When it comes to building a "seamless" brand, is there something that makes you feel uncomfortable?

Issues you wish would just disappear?

Is it time to turn a new page with your team?

"I choose to live, not just exist."   **- JAMES HETFIELD**

14
Burning the Boats

You are standing on a windswept point, gazing out over the cresting waves of the English Channel.

Surrounded by nothing but the silence of your own thoughts, you can still feel the residue of what happened more than 60 years ago. A grey morning, air dense with smoke, filled with the crack of rifle fire and the roar of cannons. Wandering along a beach once code-named "Omaha", you intuitively sense all around you, the unmistakable ghostly presence of fallen heroes.

It takes very little for you to imagine the murderious horror Allied troops had to overcome to breach the Atlantic Wall of Adolf Hitler's Fortress Europe. Machine guns screaming, artillery fire all around. How would you have reacted on that horrible day? It's impossible to predict.

June 6, 1944.

D-Day.

Given the enormity of what was at stake, those hitting the beach that morning knew one thing: there was no question of turning back. The only options for the guys on the ground were advance - or die trying. The largest invasion force in history knew, right down to the individual level, that no man could turn, run, or jump back into their crafts and hightail it back to England.

Eventually, every business owner worth his or her salt will experience what it's like to metaphorically "Burn the Boats".

"Burning the Boats" characterizes a mindset required for that moment in time when the entire fortune of your enterprise is about to be wagered in an all-or-nothing bet on a horse called Greatness. As a business owner, you are the jockey, and only you know the weight of the burden you shoulder, riding that nag mentally. While you hope and pray you wind up in the winners circle, there is still a race to be run with no guarantees of a successful outcome. Deep down, you believe in your horse. But the closer you get to the starting gate, the more knots in your gut. The more restless, sleepless nights. The more persistent that haunting echo, that whispers incessantly in your ear, "What if this doesn't work?"

Hindsight being 20/20, while many are now applauding one of the most daring and dynamic re-branding projects in Canadian business history, precious few can relate to the decision-making nightmare involved – or the burden that comes with accepting 100% responsibility for the risk involved should the best laid plans ultimately sputter and fail.

It is spring of 2007 and Ken's gut is telling him it's time for a major shift for his upstart franchise system. His business is still very much a David in a land of Goliaths. Customers and the business media have fallen in love with what his company is doing. But Ken knows in his heart it's not enough to just attract positive press. At some point, his company needs to grab a larger share of the real estate market. Nine years into a journey that began with nothing more than a big idea and less than $100 dollars, and with close to 90 franchises already in the system, Ken has a gnawing feeling that won't go away: *"Not enough people get who we really are. They still confuse us with realtors, which we're not. How do we make the masses realize we really are different?"*

Ken LeBlanc, CEO of PropertyGuys.com knows full well what is at stake. Does he listen to his instincts and ditch everything that has been done visually that allowed his company to become Canada's fastest-growing franchise system? Or, can he see through the fog of war clearly enough to face facts that, while franchise sales are healthy, overall market share is still an issue? Is it time to make a bold move to outthink and outflank one of the most competitive business categories known to mankind?

Traditional real estate and the time-honoured MLS system?

Despite the fact that PropertyGuys.com was billed as *"Your Private Sale Solution"*, the franchise was battling an overwhelming tide of public perception that they were just another realtor. Truth is, PropertyGuys.com is anything but. In 1998, Ken and co-founder Jeremy Demont created an entirely different model; a "private sale system" to help homeowners market their homes on their own, allowing sellers to negotiate directly with buyers and save thousands in real estate commissions. PropertyGuys.com was essentially "cutting out the middleman" in much the same way Michael Dell bypassed retailers to sell computers directly to his customers.

As you might expect, many realtors howled.

Nevertheless, the PropertyGuys.com message was not cutting through the commercial clutter and for months on end, Ken was consumed by thoughts that offered no clear answers.

Thoughts filled with plenty of conjecture, speculation and an endless list of "what ifs".

"Do we stay with what we've got in terms of a visual brand identity, because it has helped us get this far?"

"We could play it safe and tweak just a few things but maybe that is a risk in itself."

"Or, we could change everything and bet the farm in order to get to the next level?"

"But what if our customers don't like it? And what if our franchisees don't buy in and embrace a new look and feel?"

These are the thoughts running through the mind of a CEO responsible for providing vision and leadership to an organization about to face the biggest challenge of its ten year history. And with the 10th Anniversary conference less than eight months away, was now the time to pull the trigger on a massive brand make-over?

The facts dictated yes.

Nine out of ten people surveyed thought PropertyGuys.com was a traditional realtor. The brand Ken and his team had grown up with was in no way shape or form tied to what they actually did. Most folks had no clue that PropertyGuys.com helped them sell their homes privately. Even with a tag line stating, *"Your Private Sale Solution"*.

Emotions ran high when Ken threw an audacious alternative on the table.

Ken and his partners struggled for several weeks with a mixed bag of opinions, ideas, feelings and fears over the prospect of a complete brand makeover. It would entail not only new signs to place on customers' lawns, but a new website, marketing material, logo, colours, tag-line and advertising campaign. In effect, the only thing that would stay was the name.

In their strategy sessions, Ken, Jeremy, Dale Betts and Walter Melanson had to assess possible upsides as well as the chance they were taking. Not only was their own future at stake but they were also gambling with the future of close to a hundred franchisees. The fate of many families would hang in the balance. And if they decided to step up to the window and place the bet, the price of that ticket would be in the $500,000 dollar range.

Given a similar situation, would you "Burn the Boats"?

In the case of PropertyGuys.com, Ken and the crew decided to damn the torpedoes and launch the re-brand on a Caribbean cruise that served as the setting for an unforgettable 10th Anniversary conference. After nearly six months of complete secrecy on the size and scope of their own Operation Overlord, franchisees exploded with enthusiasm when the new signs and logo were finally unveiled during Ken's keynote address the morning of February 12th, 2008. From that moment on, PropertyGuys.com began to transform itself as a brand not only with startling new visuals, tagline and provocative radio commercials, but internally as well. About 150 people bonded over five days at sea through the course of educational sessions designed to orientate franchisees and the front-line on the essence of the new PropertyGuys.com and what it would stand for in the marketplace.

Enemy real estate agents were shrieking when the combined elements of the PropertyGuys.com ground and aerial assault hit the market in early April 2008. The round signs with their splashy colours were an instant hit, creating immediate double-takes and second looks. On the airwaves, radio listeners were asked if it was fair to list their house with a "Joe Schmo" realtor and let any windfalls go into their pockets. The new tagline delivered a direct benefit statement that eliminated any ambiguity about what PropertyGuys.com stood for. *"Sell Your House. Pay Yourself"*.

The result?

An 87% increase in 2008 listings,

91

increased market share in a number of territories, more mainstream media coverage and a surge in franchisee morale as telephones starting dancing on their desks with customers eager to learn more. Within three months of the re-brand, it was clear to Ken and his team that they were headed to the "winners circle". In fact, PropertyGuys.com became the first Atlantic Canadian company to earn the prestigious, 2008 "Award of Excellence" from the Canadian Franchise Association (CFA). And for good measure, they also earned the CFA's "Frankie Award" for their innovative brochures in the consumer retail category. Seeing the round sign show up in editorial cartoons didn't hurt either, symbolic of pop culture acceptance.

"Just as the golden arches represent fast food, we believe this round sign will be the ICON for the private sale industry."
-KEN LeBLANC, 02/12/08

"Burning the Boats" and never turning back actually originated with the 16th century Spanish explorer Hernando Cortes when he and his men hit the beaches of south-eastern Mexico. By destroying his ships, Cortes committed himself and his soldiers not only to survival but to conquer whatever obstacles came their way.

More than 500 years ago, Cortes discovered commitment is the foundation for conquering fear on the way to eventual success. Not a single race has ever been won without it. Success in business, relationships and in achieving personal goals all hinge on levels of commitment. And while the business challenges we face will never equal the magnitude of a Normandy Invasion, overcoming any barriers before us requires a similar mindset.

If you are truly serious about building a remarkable brand, what is holding you back and preventing you from acting on what your gut knows to be true?

At what point do you risk it all for the sake of an idea you truly believe in?

Are there boats in your business that needs burning?

"There is no victory at bargain basement prices."
- GENERAL DWIGHT D. EISENHOWER

15
Tale of Two Airlines

Walking up to the airline counter I can't believe my luck.

It's 8:27 a.m. and not only have I arrived more than an hour ahead of the scheduled departure time, (a feat in itself) but lo and behold, there is not a single person in front of me.

An extra bounce gets added to the step.

It happened to be one of those days when I was already cheerful, looking forward to speaking the next day at a transportation conference in Newfoundland. So with a healthy jolt of caffeine coursing through my system, and no line-up in sight, I am walking on professional sunshine.

Smiling broadly, I approach a row of four ticket agents. From about 30-feet away I exclaim in a thoroughly tongue-in-cheek, good humoured way, "So, who is going to be lucky enough to serve me today?"

Four heads – wearing the same company colours - look up from their screens.

Silence.

Not one of the frigid foursome returns the smile.

Blank looks border on stern.

And there I stood, frozen for a second that felt more like an entire minute, feeling somewhat uncomfortable, like I somehow disturbed these folks. Distracted them from something more important.

Immediately the air hisses out of my spirit balloon. Suddenly I'm feeling like that unwelcome office intruder otherwise known as the Time Burglar. *Sorry, didn't know I was interrupting.*

Walking the last ten yards, crunching invisible eggshells as I go, I arrive at the counter. In perfunctory all-business fashion, one of the senior agents reviews my documents, checks my luggage and issues a boarding pass. He matter-of-factly directs me towards security.

The other three agents resume a serious discussion amongst themselves. I grab my carry-on bag and head toward the other end of the airport. But not before passing an employee from a competing airline. She looks me square in the eye, flashes a wide grin and offers a cheery *"Good Morning"*.

Wait a second.

Did everyone from my airline miss that memo? The one that says it only takes seventeen muscles to smile and forty-three to frown.

Imagine, free air smiles. Without having to buy a thing or fill out any forms!

Several months later, a business partner is addressing a breakfast meeting of 120 human resource professionals and throws out a bold question. Darren Sears asks the group for a show of hands as to whether they would like to go to work for the first airline.

Not a single hand goes up.

Undaunted, Darren then asks how many would like to be employed with the Airline #2. Would it surprise you to know, nearly every hand shot skyward?

Is it just a coincidence that the first of these two airlines has struggled for years to turn a profit, filed for bankruptcy protection and is consistently tarred and feathered on-line and off for shoddy customer service and low employee morale? Meanwhile, Airline #2 has posted impressive financial results, (three-year average revenue growth of 105%, three-year asset growth of 85%) while earning the distinction of being "Canada's Most Admired Corporate Culture for four years running. One airline makes you feel like they're doing you a favour. The other seems genuinely pleased to see you.

In an ultra-competitive industry, surrounded by rivals that consistently hemorrhage red ink, WestJet has maintained a consistent upward trajectory of profitability and performance. West Jet is the little airline that could - and did - going from a modest start-up in 1996 with three aircraft flying to five cities, to a company of more than 65 planes and 7,200 employees, and holding the Number 4 ranking among the world's most profitable airlines. WestJet President Sean Durfy has the company on a course to gain 45% to 50% of the domestic airline market by 2013. Eight-three percent of WestJet employees are shareholders. The "People Department" attracts 1,200 unsolicited résumés weekly.

To anyone who has been a WestJet "guest", it is little wonder.

Years ago, on a business trip to British Columbia, I couldn't help but notice the consistency in attitudes and service levels between check-in and what was experienced in the cabin. From Moncton to Toronto, Toronto to Calgary, and on to Kelowna, British Columbia, the West Jet "experience" could only be described as "seamless". Treating the customer as a guest was not a hit-and-miss thing depending on who was on the front-line at the time. But more than just seamlessly consistent, the West Jet experience was also refreshingly remarkable.

Upon landing at Pearson International in Toronto, a cheerful voice announced, *"Please be careful and stay buckled up. There is always a chance we may have to stop suddenly if we get caught in traffic!"* Holy Purple Cow Batman! Talk about a difference in tone between the West Jet flight crew and their stern and emotionless competitors, who, as they lecture passengers, remind us of the grumpy teachers we have tried so hard to forget.

According to West Jet co-founder Don Bell, *"We're in the hospitality business and our culture is everything to us"*. Constructed in the mould of the wildly popular (and profitable) Southwest Airlines model in the U.S.A., West Jet has succeeded in building a brand identify from within. They recognize you can't succeed at marketing without HR and vice versa. As explained in Paul Grescoe's book *Flight Path*, Bell and his fellow West Jet founders paid close attention to what Herb Kelleher and his cohorts at Southwest were doing. As Kelleher explains, *"Any other airline can go out and get airplanes. They can acquire ticket-counter space at the terminal. They can buy baggage conveyors and uniforms. But the hardest thing for a competitor to imitate – in the customer service business - is attitude. Esprit de corps is the way the way that you treat customers and the way you feel about people. And it's very difficult to emulate that because you can't do it mechanically and you can't do it according to a formula."*

Unlike many of their competitors, West Jet recognizes "brand" is not just part of the business – it is the business. They understand the difference between a good company and a great one is in the execution of brand strategy and that little things done consistently are much more important than anything said through advertising. According to Bell, *"A brand is a promise. You can spend millions of dollars on advertising but if that flight attendant treats a customer badly, or she doesn't know what the current promotion is all about – all that money is gone. A smile is a logo too. And that's what WestJet understands better than most."*

No matter how many millions of dollars some of WestJet's competitors spend on advertising each year, most will struggle in their attempts to attract loyal customers and employees because a brand promise is something to be kept, not just made. In other words, successful branding is not just the job of the marketing department; any more than acquiring the best people is solely the responsibility of the people in HR. With a "seamless" brand - like West Jet - if magic doesn't happen on the inside, it won't be felt on the outside.

That's precisely what multiplies the emotional impact of West Jet's advertising budget. To anyone who has been a guest, you can see the tongue-in-cheek sense of humour in their television ad that leaves you chuckling; half-way believing that only a WestJetter really would track you down two days later, return a cell phone and get you $50 bucks more than the asking price for your jet ski.

As organizations face shrinking labour pools and global competition, the looming talent shortage is a primary issue discussed around many boardroom tables. However, many business leaders will struggle to see a connection between a company's culture - the brand by which it becomes known internally - and the way it performs in the market.

Do you see a problem here … or an opportunity?

For Airline #1, opportunity may have already passed it by. In February of 2009 this headline appeared in the Globe & Mail:

AIR CANADA PINS SUCCESS ON SERVICE

The story went on to indicate Air Canada's chief operating officer would be delivering cross-country pep talks urging staff to improve customer service amidst competitive threats from WestJet and the recession. Air Canada CEO Montie Brewer was reported to have sent out a three-page memo to employees, stating, "The most important factor in determining our future success is customer service. This will be the battleground this year and in the years ahead. We have a superior product and fuller network and now we need to ensure that we give each customer caring friendly service consistently — in all areas — in call centres, at the airport, in flight and dealing with any follow-up issues — to ensure that Air Canada customers remain Air Canada customers".

Suppose for a moment that you were delivering those pep talks. What would you say to those employees? How would you eradicate the all-too-frequent stares of indifference and downright sneers directed towards the only people that can keep any company in business - the customer? Does Airline #1 really have a staff motivation issue or does the problem run much deeper than that?

Are you envisioning how your company's values and guiding principles – a.k.a. corporate culture - can be a competitive advantage?

Can you imagine an environment that naturally attracts the best and brightest, willing to align their behaviour with your brand promise? And what impact would that sense of spirit and alignment have on achieving your business goals and objectives?

Several months after the Newfoundland trip, I needed to book flights to Miami and even though the price was a little more, opted for West Jet. When it was time to check-in, I discovered Nicole was originally from Prince Edward Island. To which I naturally responded, "Who's your father?" And wouldn't you know Nicole's dad and I just happened to have travelled and worked together the previous week on a project that began when we

FLIGHT PATH

HOW WESTJET IS FLYING HIGH IN CANADA'S MOST TURBULENT INDUSTRY

PAUL GRESCOE

met up with Roger and his team over in Newfoundland a few months earlier.

Maybe it's no coincidence that even in our faster, wired world, the shortest distance between two people is still a smile.

Are "Free Air Smiles" a part of what happens naturally everyday at your business?

"All the magazine ads in the world can't undo one lousy desk clerk"

-SETH GODIN

16
Selling Your "Soap"

The "Branded Networker" seminar always begins with three questions.

Who are you?

What do you do?

And, other than your own, what is your favourite brand?

In late 2008, participants from the Greater Moncton Chamber of Commerce shared their answers with people they were meeting for the first time. As is custom, some of the perennial brand favourites popped up one-by-one; Apple, Starbucks, Harley-Davidson, etc.

But, when it was Francine's turn she suggested Dove. And she didn't stop there.

Francine regaled seminar attendees with her knowledge of how Dove soap has become the champion for real beauty and how the principle behind the campaign is to celebrate natural physical differences embodied by all women and inspire them to have confidence to be comfortable in their own skin.

It was obvious to anyone listening, the branding experts behind the Dove campaign had hit one out of the park as Francine willingly (and freely) extolled the virtues of a "story" that has dramatically accelerated market share growth for the manufacturers of a bar of soap.

The Dove "Campaign for Real Beauty" is a great example of how you can heighten the perceived value of any commodity, and increase its demand simply by crafting and sharing a "story" more compelling than your competitors.

Dove focused its strategy on a universal truth. Research reveals only 2% of women worldwide consider themselves beautiful. There was near unanimous dissatisfaction around body weight and shape. And more than two-thirds of women agreed media and advertising had set unrealistic standards of beauty, with models weighing, on average, 23 percent less than the average woman.

The Dove message cut through the clutter and BS of the beauty industry, by confronting a dirty little secret: You can't sell a beauty product without somehow playing on women's insecurities. If women thought they looked perfect—just the way they are—why would they buy anything?

By taking an entirely different, counterintuitive approach, the Dove campaign got noticed in a hurry when it was launched in 2004 as the debate went mainstream with Oprah and Ellen before 30 million daytime TV viewers. "Real Beauty" struck a nerve with women who were sick of bullshit marketing exhorting them to look like anorexic airbrushed models.

"Because there is a natural storytelling urge and ability in all human beings, even just a little nurturing of this impulse can bring about astonishing and delightful results"
                    - NANCY MELLON, The Art of Storytelling

Dove kept the campaign going, launching the Dove Self-Esteem Fund in 2006 as customers continue to buy this "story" in almost every key market across the globe. Worldwide sales of the Dove brand increased by about 13%, an astronomical figure in the highly competitive packaged goods industry.

In the end, both beauty and truth may be in the eye of the beholder. But as you reflect right now on your product or service and the customer you serve, consider this:

Have you been focused on just "selling the soap"? Or do you have a compelling "story" that supports it?

In other words, does your branding message tend to focus more on the actual "soap" - the product or service you sell - or have you figured out a "story" that would actually matter to a customer that cares? Is there a universal truth about your product or service you could begin to tell a customer who would pay to fall in love with your story - and spread the good word?

If beauty is only spin deep, how does the timeless principle of "storytelling" apply to your business and your brand?

"Why was Solomon recognized as the wisest man in the world? Because he knew more stories (proverbs) than anyone else. Scratch the surface in a typical boardroom and we're all just cavemen with briefcases, hungry for a wise person to tell us stories"
- ALAN KAY, VP, Walt Disney Co.

Side Three

17. Advertising Artillery

18. The Blizzard of Brand

19. Bad Medicine

20. Brand Candy

21. Crocodiles Rock

22. Rays of Human Sunshine

23. Branding in a Brilliant Disguise

24. Messing with Words

25. Something Different

26. Who's Teaching Who

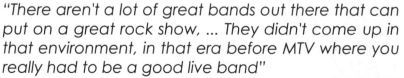

"There aren't a lot of great bands out there that can put on a great rock show, ... They didn't come up in that environment, in that era before MTV where you really had to be a good live band"

- JOE PERRY

17
Advertising Artillery

It's an otherwise ordinary Friday morning at a local gym.

Some would say this gym is really a singles bar that doesn't serve alcohol. And while that may be true for the office crowd that heads over after work, I'm fairly convinced only those with nothing on their mind but fitness would show up before the ungodly hour of 6:00 a.m.

These are focused types.

Eyes straight ahead. No idle chit-chat. People on a mission. Hostilities resuming in a personal war waged against a constantly moving target of an enemy - those 10-15 extra pounds.

For me this morning, the battle unfolds on the weaponry of a state-of-the art elliptical machine that provides real-time feedback on heart rate, caloric burn and miles travelled. The local classic rock station provides a soundtrack to sweat by, blaring in from wall-mounted speakers.

About 10 minutes into the mission, the groove being laid down by Aerosmith is interrupted by radio commercials that fire in like enemy howitzers. At 6:22 a.m. reports indicate Local Car Dealer #1 is presenting the "Sales Event of the Decade" under a gigantic tent and 200 vehicles MUST go before the weekend was up.

Sounds like they weren't taking any prisoners on that one.

After Bono's musical confession about not finding what he is looking for, the next salvo began at precisely 6:34 a.m. with Local Dealer #2 informing us the once-a-year "Annual Clearance Sale" was now on (with many makes and models to choose from!). And once Van Halen inspired us to "Jump", the next commercial island pounded us with an "Inventory Blow-out Sale" from Local Car Dealer #3 - This weekend only! Zero money down! All vehicles below factory invoice!

Welcome to the radio advertising version of trench warfare where they grind 'em up and spit 'em out. Advertisers buy the bullets. Copy writers load the cannons. Announcers fire the machine guns. Audiences duck and run for cover.

This is what is referred to as a "spray & pray" strategy.

Not that there is anything wrong with that.

Not as long as it's not your money buying the ammo.

This strategy is by no means restricted to radio or the automotive sector. It could just as easily be newspaper ads or television commercials serving as a rocket launcher for whatever message you hope will find its target. Sadly, millions of dollars (perhaps some of yours?) are being sacrificed in local advertising markets across North America daily, in futile efforts to bridge the no man's land that exists between a business and the mind field of a customer.

Wanna know how to win this war?

It's simple. You do one of two things:

1.) Withdraw. Find a new battlefield. Avoid the financial bloodbath. Sun Tzu himself stated that there was no dishonour in leaving a fight you can't win.

2.) Stay. Unleash new verbal weaponry – based on a revitalized and remarkable brand promise. Weaponry that will render your competitors helpless. Leave them reeling with shock and awe. Some will be forced to wave the white flag of surrender.

Unmistakable patterns have emerged in many local advertising markets as companies spend billions of dollars to scream in our ears. Telling us how much better and different they are compared to the other guys down the street. It reminds one of General Douglas Haig's strategy to incur 420,000 casualties at the Battle of the Somme in 1916 in a bloody effort to gain a paltry 7 miles of French real estate.

Why fight that type of war when today's customer is immune to "ad-speak"?

Customers are ignoring the language of hype in greater numbers every day (which is great as long as your competitors are paying for it!).

So let's go back to the first option.

You could create an entirely new marketing playing field, inviting only those customers you most want to engage. In their ground-breaking book *Blue Ocean Strategy*, authors W. Chan Kim and Renee Mauborgone pinpointed two strategic playing fields:

1). **"Red Oceans"** = Defined and accepted industry boundaries with vast numbers of competitors outslugging each other for market share, bloodying the water with hefty ad budgets that trumpet price-driven commodities leading to shrinking profit margins and minimal growth.

2). **"Blue Oceans"** = Uncontested market space ripe and unlimited ceilings for growth as companies create a "category of one". Some of the best examples include Cirque du Soleil's blending of opera & ballet with a circus format that eliminates animals. Or Curves fitness centres - which created a new space for women between traditional gyms and home exercise programs. In a "blue ocean, your company swims alone, discovering un-chartered waters with higher margins, loyal customers and profitable growth.

The second option will hinge on your ability to actually craft a promise around a strategy that delivers something that matters to your customer. Something relevant. Unexpected. And most importantly, something believable

Marketing messages, built on a rock solid brand promise, become your new weaponry. They are your version of the British tanks introduced in the latter stages of World War One. While everyone else is still flinging grenades from foxholes, you are cutting through the clutter, smashing through the tangled mess of barbed wire, navigating minefields and crushing anything else in your way as your market offensive gathers momentum. Your message is based on unshakeable principles. Principles that serve as the "values mountain" you are fully prepared to plant a flag on and defend to your death.

We're talking about the kind of stuff you have thought long and hard about.

Even anguished over.

Perhaps it's why you started the business in the first place. Once you have conquered that territory and have clarity about what your brand stands for (and against) you can develop an armour-plated advertising message, designed to slice through the "white noise" of the marketplace.

And this approach can work for any business in any category.

If you were to pull back the curtain, you would discover similar branding principles at work in Apple's hugely successful "I'm a Mac" campaign or at a small business like Jim Gilbert's Wheels & Deals of Fredericton, NB, gaining national acclaim as *"Canada's Huggable Car Dealer"*. In Apple's case, brand essence centres on all things "cool" and the controversial *"I'm a Mac"* campaign drove that message home with staggering effectiveness. As far as Jim Gilbert the car dealer was concerned, all of his competitors looked and sounded pretty much the same with over-hyped, testosterone-fuelled advertising. Jim focussed his campaign on humorous, whimsical 30-second vignettes painting him as the "Romeo of Roadsters and the "McDreamy of Drive". In both campaigns, the contrast was clear to anyone watching or listening - and so were the business results.

By building a remarkable brand, based on strong emotional triggers, Fortune 500 giants and small-town companies can capture the imagination of customers they most want to reach. And it doesn't matter whether you are catering to the cool crowd who reject anything that smacks of being "square" or warm-hearted folks who value relationships as opposed to transactional, tire-kicking, bargain-hunting goobers shopping on price.

Is there anything preventing your brand from doing the same thing?

Aren't you just like your customers?

Living in a world of too many options with too little time? Anything that ain't solving a problem or making you money gets mentally tossed aside.

You ignore ordinary stuff. But you wish you had more customers.

Your biggest challenge when it comes to getting your brand noticed is becoming worthy of attention in the first place. In other words, what is it that your business does that truly deserves to be labelled as uncommonly "remarkable"? Seth Godin, author ten best-selling books, refers to the concept as being a "Purple Cow"; defined as offering a product or service that is - remarkable. Seth contends that if you were driving along a country road, passing farm after farm, the brown and black cows would eventually start to look the same. But a "Purple Cow" would be noticed right away. Who knows you might even stop and pose for a picture.

Few companies, however, fall into the "Purple Cow" category.

In our experience, it's definitely less than 10%. Maybe even less than 5%.

There are only four slots in any business category. Your brand will fit into one of the other three, unless you are one of those rare individuals who have invested the time and resources to create an uncommonly remarkable, "Purple Cow" type of brand. For the record, the other three slots are decided by the way consumers spend their money each day. They are as follows:

1. "Better than average" - a few companies who are good at what they do.
2. "Average" - the majority, who you can take or leave.
3. "Mediocre" - a few, barely scraping by, hoping no one notices or complains.

If you operate a small to medium-sized business, the slot marked "remarkable" is well within your grasp.

And while you may think branding is the sole domain of the Fortune 500 world, small businesses everywhere are starting to see the wisdom, that to be heard, you need BE uncommonly remarkable to separate yourself from the herd.

Much will depend on how you, as Supreme Allied Commander, want your brand to be perceived and received. How much thought has been given to allocating your marketing resources so that you gain ground while minimizing losses? In what way does your brand strategy prevent your advertising budget from becoming a casualty of a "Ready-Aim-Fire", "Duck-and-Pray" philosophy?

Meanwhile, it's Monday morning at the gym.

Back in the iron jungle, resuming the elliptical grind to sonic blasts of Guns N Roses and at precisely 6:47 a.m., we learn the "Sales Event of the Decade" promised by Car Dealer #1 was being held over for another week. Seems like all 200 vehicles didn't have to go by Sunday at six after all.

Despite what the ads implied, heavens did not collide.

The earth continued to spin on its axis.

But it was anything but quiet on radios western front.

"The more you sweat in peace, the less you bleed in war"

-GENERAL DOUGLAS MacARTHUR

18
The Blizzard of Brand

It was the first snowstorm of the year and boy, was it a biggie!

More than 50 centimetres piling up relentlessly, mercilessly. A punishing, whiteout keeping most vehicles cowering in snow swept driveways throughout Maritime Canada.

If not for a prescription that needed refilling at a nearby drug store, Peter and Julie would never have dared venture out in such hazardous conditions. And a short two minute drive to the pharmacy - that became a 25 minute ordeal - convinced them they should hurry back home. The driving was just too treacherous.

However, they decided to make what they thought would be a quick, second stop, at a nearby Tim Horton's coffee shop across the street from the pharmacy. Julie needs a coffee to warm her chilled bones – she'd just spent a couple of hours outside shovelling. The drive-thru was backed-up, and there appeared to be little, if any, in-store traffic, so Peter offered to run inside lickety-split while Julie waited, huddled in the car.

And she waited.

The blowing snow and howling wind swirling outside her icy windows only served to escalate Julie's growing frustration. No sign of Peter. "What's taking him so long?" she wondered. Finally, after a 20-minute wait that felt more like two hours, Peter returned with her coffee.

And an explanation.

Turns out, there were only two other people ahead of him and as Peter exchanged pleasantries with the man directly in front, conversation naturally turned to the weather. The man – decked out in snappy company apparel – casually mentioned he wasn't bothered in the least by the havoc this storm had created. After all, he had just roared off the lot with a new four-wheel drive vehicle from a nearby dealership where he worked as a car salesman. He explained he had a large order to place for him and his co-workers and since the inclement weather had brought business to a standstill, he jumped at the chance to make this coffee run.

Just as casually, Peter mentioned he was just there to buy a single coffee for his wife out waiting in the car. The salesman chuckled, "Tough!" as he bellied up to the server, whipping out his lengthy, written list with about 15 coffee orders as well as a number of other items, bagels, sandwiches and a box of Timbits. By this time, there were only two customers in the shop - Peter and the salesman.

Standing and waiting for the large order to be filled.

No further words were exchanged.

Awkward silence spoke volumes.

When a shivering Julie heard what had happened, her blood mercury boiled over. Beyond incredulous; she couldn't believe anyone would be that inconsiderate and downright rude, much less someone whose livelihood depended on sales. She vowed never to set foot on the lot and buy a vehicle from that dealership. Peter, ever the loving husband, nodded in agreement.

Ironically, this particular dealership invests about $250,000 annually in local advertising. Hoping and praying that people like Peter and Julie visit their lot and give their sales team a chance to move inventory. Repeated studies have shown brand loyalty is impacted by as much as 80% by what happens at the three-foot radius between customer and front-line as opposed to anything being advertised on a 30-foot billboard. No amount of great marketing, terrific products and everyday low prices can save a brand sabotaged by some jerk wearing the company uniform. Inside the building or out of the office, if any front-liner fails – everything fails. Any positive effect from any dollar invested in ads, location and training melts faster than a snowflake on a July afternoon.

The salesman in question benefit from knowing that he is already battling incredible odds from the get-go. Within 12 months of a vehicle purchase, consumers told a National Research Survey:

- 92% of them did not receive a proper product presentation
- 93% of salespeople failed to follow-up
- 89% believed their sales person lacked product knowledge

Also interesting to note is the #1 reason why most people *did* make a decision to buy:

- 91% indicated there was a *genuinely, helpful, salesperson.*

Does this revelation surprise you?

Would you believe, when all things are equal, people still like to buy from people they like, know and trust? Even when things like price aren't equal, people will still buy from those they like know and trust. However the opposite is also true. And in this category it's even more critical to build relationships at ground zero because brand loyalty surpasses dealer loyalty. More than half of consumers will likely purchase or lease the same BMW, Toyota, Honda, Volvo or Mercedes or other vehicle they currently own, while less than 40% will buy from the same dealer.

Given the fact this salesman was draped in company attire, he was obviously unaware of potential disconnects in the minds of potential future customers like Peter and Julie. In effect, he kissed off two prospects, their circle of friends, generated negative word-of-mouth (that could turn viral) while killing the potential effect of thousands of ad dollars the dealership was spending to communicate a folksy, homespun image.

A great brand is built on much more than catchy taglines, flashy colours or hot sounding radio spots. Great marketing starts from the inside, from the way we answer the phone, to the way we "wear" the brand. These are just some of the "little things' that make a world of difference between someone in "sales" and a "sales professional".

In ultra-competitive business environments, everything matters. "Little things" don't mean a lot - they mean everything!

While it's easy to point fingers and place blame on the shoulders of some poor sales schmuck, the story does raise some interesting and provocative questions about the potential for similar brand disconnects in any organization:

- Do your people behave one way when they're "on the job" and represent the company in a different fashion when they're off the clock?
- Are your people *seamlessly* aligned with your brand or are there glaring differences between what the ads portray and what actually happens face-to-face? Are your employees really that "friendly and knowledgeable?
- Should the opinions and feelings of future customers be casually dismissed because what you are selling is in such high demand that current customers will drive through raging snowstorms just to buy from you?

There is a world of difference between doing a job and delivering a brand.

However, in fairness to the front-line, precious few organizations recognize the value in creating the kind of environment that fosters a culture and a brand that lives outside the four walls, at backyard barbecues, cocktail parties and coffee shop line-ups.

Want to get serious about managing the entire brand experience?

Start with the low hanging fruit: employee orientation and training. Most customer-facing employees don't receive any training on how to represent their brand in public. What most companies call "training" focuses on product features, work procedures and compliance, delivered with text-heavy PowerPoint presentations accompanied by the drowsiness-inducing monotone of sterile canned speeches.

How clear has your brand essence and promise been communicated to the people who need to know it the most? Has that message been delivered in an engaging, fun, interactive format suited for the iPod generation?

Business owners always have a choice; either align your frontline with what the brand represents or cross your fingers and hope your people will plough ahead and figure it out on their own.

"I heard that chivalry was dead, but I think it's just got a bad flu"   **-MEG RYAN**

19
Bad Medicine

Imagine selling a product or service that blatantly advertises its shortcomings.

Buckley's Mixture adopted that brand strategy more than two decades ago with its promise...

"It tastes awful. And it works."

Buckley's Mixture has tasted horrible since it was developed by W.K. Buckley, a Toronto pharmacist, in 1919. He discovered several natural ingredients used in the treatment of coughs and colds (the recipe is a closely guarded company secret) combining them to create a signature product. By the mid-1980s, and with sales lagging, Buckley's son Frank decided on a new campaign that trumpeted its truly awful taste and remarkable healing powers. The strategy worked. Buckley's won several advertising awards, gained significant market share and sales surged, lifting brand value with it.

Don't you feel a certain level of admiration for brands that have no qualms about stating it the way it is? Buckley's isn't for everyone. And they have stuck to their guns, even though they've been pressured to introduce a better tasting mixture. Of course, if Buckley's didn't actually work, all that taste-bud torture would be for naught and the product wouldn't sell. In other words, this brand has the gonads to deliver on its promise - warts and all.

And would you believe Buckley's customers don't mind one bit?

In fact, an invitation to show the world exactly how bad this stuff tastes, had consumers responding in droves to an Internet campaign asking them to try Buckley's and send in pictures and videos through MySpace and YouTube of the awful faces they make. Another series of ads featured comparative taste testing between Buckley's and various awful alternatives including

Spring Break Hot Tub Water, Used Mouthwash, Public Restroom Puddle, Trash Bag Leakage, Pig Tongue Scrapings and Cardio Workout Perspiration.

The Buckley's brand (now owned by Novartis) has succeeded in creating a brand position as the 'no frills' solution for people who just want to stop their cough. Simply sharing the truth and being real makes it impossible for any other brand in their category to copy.

Another brand that sees the wisdom in keeping it real is the web-based, mega-brand Google. Not so much from a marketing perspective, but more from what they actually DO in serving their customers. Here is part of an e-mail sent out recently, (August 27, 2008 to be exact), to a friend of mine who happens to be a Google Apps customer.

We're committed to making Google Apps Premier Edition a service on which your organization can depend. During the first half of August, we didn't do this as well as we should have. We had three outages - on August 6, August 11, and August 15. The August 11 outage was experienced by nearly all Google Apps Premier users while the August 6 and 15 outages were minor and affected a very small number of Google Apps Premier users. As is typical of things associated with Google, these outages were the subject of much public commentary. Through this note, we want to assure you that system reliability is a top priority at Google. When outages occur, Google engineers around the world are immediately mobilized to resolve the issue. We made mistakes in August, and we're sorry. While we're passionate about excellence, we can't promise you a future that's completely free of system interruptions. Instead, we promise you rapid resolution of any production problem; and more importantly, we promise you focused discipline on preventing recurrence of the same problem. Given the production incidents that occurred in August, we'll be extending the full SLA credit to all Google Apps Premier customers for the month of August, which represents a 15-day extension of your service. SLA credits will be applied to the new service term for accounts with a renewal order pending. This credit will be applied to your account automatically so there's no action needed on your part. We've also heard your guidance around the need for better communication when outages occur. Here are three things that we're doing to make things better....

Once again, thanks for you continued support and understanding.

Sincerely,

The Google Apps Team

Google, according to the 2008 BrandZ rankings, was valued at $86 billion making it the world's top brand for the second year in a row. Better than General Electric, Microsoft, Coca-Cola and China Mobile. Even more remarkable, is when you consider Google became a household name without spending a dime on advertising. Electing to build their brand on a foundation of culture, Google has been identified many times as the #1 Best Place to Work by Fortune Magazine. The unofficial company slogan is "Don't be Evil".

Mark Twain was once quoted as saying, *"Always tell the truth. That way, you don't have to remember what you said"*. Great brands achieve their greatness by displaying courage to tell the truth. And in this age of universal deception, hidden agendas and exaggerated claims, simply telling the truth sets your brand apart as somewhat revolutionary.

Legendary advertising guru Bill Bernbach may have captured it best when he opined, *"Here is a great gimmick, let's tell the truth"*. Bernbach successfully applied that philosophy throughout his career which included award-winning campaigns such as Volkswagen's "Think Small" and "We Try Harder" from Avis. Bill felt that no matter how skilful you are, you can't invent a product advantage that doesn't exist. And if you do, and it's just a gimmick, it's going to fall apart anyway.

In the case of Avis, in 1962, Hertz was the clear leader in the car rental business. Avis was back in the pack, an unprofitable company with 11% of the U.S. market. Within a year of launching the "We Try Harder" campaign Avis was in the black and by 1966, had tripled its market share to 35%.

Bad medicine can be good business.

Don't you admire people and brands a lot more when they have the balls to give it to you straight, sparing you candy-coated bullshit? Are there other brands you've noticed that do a bang-up job delivering the unvarnished truth? Do you find it to be such a rare thing, that you are delighted to tell it?

Dig deep enough and you may discover a way to distinguish your brand from all others, simply by revealing a believable and compelling strength – especially if it stings a little at first.

Is there a way your brand could leverage painful truths about your business?

Think this truth thing would spread virally?

"Your love is like bad medicine, bad medicine is what I need" **-JON BON JOVI**

20
Brand Candy

"And to make this seminar even more comfortable, we have bowls of M&M candies available ... with the brown ones removed for your protection".

With that one line several years ago, intense curiosity began brewing in the brains of about 75 people attending *"The Branded Networker"* at a regional conference. Since the program was split over two days, attendees were kept somewhat in suspense, to the point where people would approach the seminar leader out of the blue at the evening social, offering theories to explain the M&M mystery. For the first time in conference history, there were more attendees on the second day of the education session. Over 100 people showed up for the last half of *"The Branded Networker"* and solved the puzzle of the "Brown M&M's".

It wasn't anything these insurance types expected.

Not even close.

As any serious fan of the rock group Van Halen can tell you, the standard performance contract during their glory days in the late 70's and early '80s included a provision calling for the band to be provided backstage with (among other things) bowls of M&M candies, but with all the brown ones removed. The 53-page document also stipulated promoters supply "herring in sour cream," four cases of "Schlitz Malt Liquor beer and one large tube KY Jelly." Lead singer David Lee Roth explained the method behind the madness in his autobiography, *Crazy from the Heat:*

"The contract rider read like a version of the Chinese Yellow Pages because there was so much equipment, and so many human beings to make it function. So just as a little test, in the technical aspect of the rider, it would say "Article 148: There will be fifteen amperage voltage sockets at twenty-foot spaces,

evenly, providing nineteen amperes" This kind of thing. And article number 126, in the middle of nowhere, was: "There will be no brown M&M's in the backstage area, upon pain of forfeiture of the show, with full compensation." So, when I would walk backstage, if I saw a brown M&M in that bowl, well, line-check the entire production. Guaranteed you're going to arrive at a technical error. They didn't read the contract. Guaranteed you'd run into a problem. Sometimes it would threaten to destroy the whole show."

The magnitude of myopic detail is flying off the drum riser.

We're talking candy with a caveat from a front man who once claimed he was a part of Americana as much as the Nike swoosh or McDonalds Golden Arches.

Diamond Dave may have more in common with Phillip Knight and Ray Kroc than he realizes. Knight, the former Nike chairman has been known to obsess over the English classes he attends at Stanford University, including "English 95: Form and Theory of the Novel". The billionaire Knight, who aspires to become a novelist, routinely buries himself in details of homework assignments that focus on topics such as Hemingway, and the 1926 novel "The Sun Also Rises". Meanwhile, Kroc, who founded the world's largest fast-food franchise, would pay riveting attention to even the smallest of details. From the storage and cooking temperatures of the French fries, to the exact shape of the hamburger patties, to the precise time it took to deliver both, no detail went overlooked. Leaving no wrapper unturned, Kroc would even go to his rivals' outlets and sift through their garbage can in order to determine which product lines were selling poorly and thus being thrown out.

However, no one ever took attention to detail to a higher level than Walter and a vision that manifested from a Florida swamp.

On the day of the Kennedy assassination in 1963, Walt flies over a 27,000 acre tract of land near Orlando and sees magic. Three years later, he passes on to another kingdom, but younger brother Roy ensures Walt's dream comes true with an official opening, October 1, 1971.

"Get a good idea and stay with it. Dog it, and work it until it's done and done right" **-WALT DISNEY**

Walt believed there was no such thing as an insignificant detail. Every corner of the Magic Kingdom bears witness to that belief. At Walt Disney World, no stone is left unturned in the effort to make magic happen in each and every one of more than 2.5 billion customer contacts that occur each year.

It begins with talent.

There are more than 57,000 employees with Disney rejecting two out of every three applicants for front-line entry-level positions. More than 99 resumes are rejected for each salaried job. Cast members that pass the "Traditions" program and advance to the front line must strictly adhere to Disney's goals - or else. Cast members who receive three reprimands in a year see the curtain close on their Disney career.

Disney cast members are never seen "out of character" as tunnels are used to get around undetected. All landscaping and repair work is done at night. Seven and a half tons of laundry is cleaned each hour and Mickey Mouse himself has 175 different sets of duds ranging from a scuba suit to a tuxedo. Chambermaids are trained to arrange stuffed animals to face the door of a hotel room, so they appear to greet kids returning from the park. Every piece of trash is separated and recycled. Decorative waste cans are never more than 25 paces away from any spot in the park. The most frequently asked question from guests is *What time is the three o'clock parade"*?

When guests complained they could not get around the daily parade to take advantage of shorter lines at some of the most popular rides, Disney spent more than $26-million to build a bridge that circumvented the parade route. Disney knew that without the bridge, the number of complaints would only grow. Rides are multi-million dollar tangible pieces of machinery that take years to engineer and construct, but Disney pays even more attention to non-tangibles such as time it takes to park car, how long it takes to buy tickets, how much it costs to buy food and merchandise, as well as wait in line times and how guests are handled when asking for directions.

Paying attention to "Brown M&M's" helps Disney achieve repeat visitor rates of more than 70%. Hotel occupancy is more than 90%.

"Brown M&M's" is a metaphor that serves as an example of how unique signatures can be attached to otherwise everyday, mundane things you do in your business. It also speaks volumes about paying strict attention to the tiniest of details that impact your brand experience – in a way you can have fun with!

Are there branding signals you could create in an effort to make product or service delivery even more "magical"?

Are "Brown M&M's" an idea you can "Jump" on and trigger an "Eruption" of brand intensity??

Van Halen's 2007/08 reunion tour with the customer-focused, detail-obsessed Roth grossed more than 93 million dollars, making it their most successful tour in a 30-year history. It was the first tour with 16 year-old bassist Wolfgang Van Halen on board joining his father, guitar gunslinger Eddie Van Halen and uncle, powerhouse drummer Alex Van Halen. Nearly one million fans went "Runnin' with the Devil" during the 74 arena shows and history repeated itself in Detroit when Wolfgang requested "no Brown M&M's" in his dressing room as a tribute to his dad. The caterer ensured all brown ones were then placed in a bowl and left in Eddie's dressing room.

"You come to the planet with nothing and you leave with nothing, so you'd better do some good while you are here" **-ALEX VAN HALEN**

21
Crocodiles Rock

Are there only two kinds of people in your world?

Ponder for a moment and see where this takes us...

Have you noticed in your travels, business dealings, relationships and life experiences, there are?:

Givers and takers?

Doers and slackers?

Lovers and fighters?

Heroes and villains?

Innovators and imitators?

Walkers and talkers?

Canadiens lovers and Habs haters?

(If you're an American, replace Canadiens with Yankees, Lakers or Cowboys and you'll get the picture).

When it comes to professional wrestling, have you noticed there is a group of people who need no explanation in terms of "getting it"; while on the other side there are folks for whom no explanation will ever do?

Have you also noticed same dualistic pattern when it comes to choices people make regarding footwear?

Specifically, "Crocs"?

Personally, I can't stand them. I fall into the *"you couldn't pay me enough to wear them"* category, but for a brand like Crocs that's a good thing. In other words, thanks to people like me, the folks who own a brand like that are giggling, chortling and laughing all the way to the bank. Whether you are in love with Crocs or not, should not detract from what this brand has accomplished since taking its first awkward steps, when three Colorado honky cats were cheering themselves up on a Caribbean booze cruise.

Was it the tequila that made them madmen across the water?

It 2002, Scott Seaman, Duke Hanson and George Baedeker headed out on a sailboat to drown their blues and share a few brews and business ideas. Baedeker had become a self-made millionaire from pizza franchising. He had a soft heart and a drinking challenge, and had invited Hanson, a childhood friend and marketing guy, out on the boat with him that day. Hanson was on a bit of a losing streak: he'd lost his job, his mother, and his wife had filed for divorce. Now in recovery mode, Hanson had moved into the "Dejected Man House" with another recently separated guy, electronics exec, Ron Snyder.

Three men in a boat - about to have a life altering experience.

Once at sea, Scott showed his down-on-their-luck buddies a new, Canadian-made boat shoe.

"The first thing I said was, 'Man, are those ugly!' recalls Hanson.

But then he tried them on.

"It was like walking on Nerf Balls".

Unlike other clogs, this shoe was cool and lightweight. Slip- and smell-resistant. (The resin is "closed cell," which means bacteria can't take root.) The partners promptly struck a U.S. licensing agreement with Quebec-based Foam Creations.

The guys thought "Foam Creations" lacked a certain ring. Hanson stepped up with a new name. He was keen on crocodiles because they're good on both land and water, live a long time, and have no natural predators. Then he realized that when the shoe is viewed from the side, it slopes up like a crocodile's snout.

Eureka!

"Crocs" were born.

The newly christened Crocs were a hit at the 2002 Fort Lauderdale boat show, where the first 1000 pairs sold out in three days. Hanson knew they were on to something big when the fire marshal started yelling that the crowd gathered around their booth was blocking the aisles. Hanson was tossing pairs of the colourful shoes at passers-by, asking them to slip them on:

"People would say, 'Man, those are ugly,' and we would say, 'You just got to try them on.'"

Crocs were an even bigger hit as retail and sales agents started snapping them up at the March 2003 Shoe Market of the Americas footwear exhibition. From there, popularity mushroomed. Sales poured in. By the end of 2003, Crocs were well on their way to becoming a bona-fide phenomenon, universally accepted as an all purpose shoe for comfort and fashion.

As demand exploded, Crocs Inc. acquired Foam Creations in June 2004, and in February 2006, it went public. The "Dejected Men" have done well for themselves. Sales climbed to $840 million in 2007. Snyder has been CEO of Crocs since 2005 and shepherded the shoe brand through its IPO with a market value that currently exceeds $1 billion.

More than 5,300 employees are now employed at Crocs operations that span the globe. The firm operates manufacturing facilities in Mexico, Brazil, and Italy, while suppliers in Asia, Europe, and the US make the rest with the products available through reputable retailers such as Dillard's, Nordstrom, and The Sports Authority,

Despite the goofy appearance, Crocs drew many accolades for comfort. (As one blogger put it, *"You have to put on a pair and try them and, I swear, you won't care if they look like donkey balls, you'll just love them."*) But there are also a significant number of Croc haters out there as witnessed by the website http://www.ihatecrocs.com/ (*Dedicated to the elimination of Crocs and those who think that their excuses for wearing them are viable*).

Such is the price one pays for developing an irresistible magnetic brand.

If you gaze down your yellow brick road and hope to see a brand with magnetic appeal in your future, consider this:

magnetic / mag'netik / adj. 1 having the properties of a magnet. 2 producing or acting by magnetism. 3 very attractive or alluring (a magnetic personality).

By its very definition, the strength of any magnet only ever equals the degree in which it repels that which it does not attract. In other words, many great brands have determined a repellent factor must exist in order for a brand to attract and hold on to loyal customers. Brands as diverse as Apple, World Wrestling Entertainment and Crocs have proven the product they sell is less important than the brand they market, but in doing so, each is making a choice - knowing they can't be all things to all people.

Magnetic brands are enhanced by more than a little "drama".

Drama is why the Leafs, Red Sox, Redskins and Celtics sell more tickets (and achieve higher scalper prices) when the Canadiens, Yankees, Cowboys and Lakers are in town.

It's also why the more their primary competitor is portrayed as a "square", the "cooler" Apple becomes. Creating conditions and taking a position that inspires polar opposites helps explain the staggering success of the "I'm a Mac" campaign, as well as understanding why legions of Croc fans endure endless ridicule, wearing shoes that make them look so ridiculous. But none of this success happens unless three "Dejected Men" are bold enough to bet the farm on a brand strategy that dared position their product as "comfortably ugly" - a big idea that became a magnetic north for the business. Setting a course for what they should and shouldn't do.

Are you getting a sense of what it takes to shake off the business "herd mentality" and do things no one else would dare?

In the mid-eighties, Vince McMahon thumbed his nose at convention and built a national brand on the theatrics and showmanship of professional wrestling. The strategy hinged on breaking an unwritten rule that twenty or so regional promoters who controlled U.S. wrestling "territories" wouldn't compete with each other. But McMahon bucked tradition and began paying local TV stations to broadcast tapes of their company's wrestling matches. McMahon believed he could build a nationwide audience for stars like "Hulk Hogan" and "Macho Man Savage", even if it meant stepping on the toes of the people who owned what amounted to personal fiefdoms. Decades later, the WWE still offends as many as it attracts as it continues to grow as a brand. As McMahon once put it, *"The worst sound in our business is silence. That means they don't care"*.

What sounds are you hearing in your business?

An overabundance of look-alike products and me-too services, is forcing customers to search for something, *anything* that is even remotely different.

Have you determined how to separate your "Crocs" from the clutter? Are you ready for your brand to be so different that, in effect, you would be ready to choose who to lose? If so, you could begin by making a list of all of the specific qualities that define your product or service:

Big or small?
Spirited or solemn?
Pricey or dirt cheap?
Durable or disposable?
Local or global?
Plain or "purple"?
Reckless or methodical?
Pragmatic or ethereal?
Heavenly beautiful or hideously ugly?

Which of these or other qualities can give your brand its sharpest focus? What stops you from developing a list that would clearly set your brand apart from any and all competitors?

It takes courage to be a little different. It takes a lot of courage to be very different. But courage is where success is found. For every branding home run hitters like Crocs, there are hundreds of "woulda-coulda-shouldas" that have struck out, shuffled back to the dugout and sat down for a lack of courage.

What makes a brand confident or brave?

The first is when a brand can actually back its claims. Not only make promises - but keep them. The second is when a brand is willing to focus on the values and the big idea that bring the brand alive, rather than just bringing in revenue. The third is when a brand dares to take a tightly focused, narrow-minded stand, even if it finds itself alone and out on a limb.

Want to broaden the audience appeal of your brand?

Magnetize and galvanize fans, followers, believers and unashamed worshipers?

Narrow your focus.

"The great thing about rock and roll is that someone like me can be a star." **-ELTON JOHN**

22
Rays of Human Sunshine

From the Grande Dame of Brand

Entering the trade show area, I turn left and begin walking down the far aisle.

And there, in the distance, she appears in full view.

Live and in living colour.

A legend I had heard about and read about.

One of those people we tend to admire from afar.

And now, quickly recovering from a momentary lapse of starstruckedness, I'm about to march right over and introduce myself to a woman who has been a source of inspiration for entrepreneurs everywhere.

Her story leaves you shaking your head in wonder.

"How in the heck did she pull that off?"

Born in a small town on the Gaspe Peninsula in Quebec, Cora grew up poor and had dreams of becoming a writer. She recalls, "Figured I would become a teacher and then jump into writing."

After attending just two years of university, majoring in classical languages and literature, she married at the age of 21. Soon she was a full-time housewife and mother to three children.

But after 13 years, Cora's husband exited the scene, leaving her with three young children, no money and no job. No employer would hire her. Many called her overqualified.

"At 40 I found myself alone and I had to do something. Studying I guess didn't teach a trade to earn a living, so I sold the family house and opened a little snack bar. Not because I wanted to do a big breakfast chain, I didn't even know about it, but I just needed to feed my kids and what I loved was cooking."

Left to her own devices, she opened her first small neighbourhood restaurant in 1980 and quickly discovered a passion for customer service. In short order, vast numbers of diners were lining up and filling her eatery daily, tripling its value.

In 1987 she bought a small abandoned snack bar in Montreal's St-Laurent area and decided to focus solely on breakfast. Combining fresh fruit, cheeses, cereal, omelettes, crêpes, waffles and French toast, she soon had customers scrambling to sample her novel morning menu.

"When I was young, I wanted to do things in business, but I thought entrepreneurs had to be unique people with special gifts. I think that they are ordinary people who have extraordinary persistence." "Whenever people ask what made me a businesswoman, I always say it was the business that did it. The same way the first child she brings into the world turns a woman into a mother, so my first restaurant turned me into a boss."

How did she do it?

What secret ingredient allowed her to go from heartache to heartstrong?

When pressed for an answer, Cora Tsouflidou can summarize it in one word.

Passion.

The passion she holds for the business itself, the customers it serves and the passion she shares with the people who have helped her build a nationwide chain, spreading its own brand of sunshine from coast-to-coast. As of this printing, Cora's passion and commitment has inspired a family of no fewer than 96 restaurants with expansion plans for 100 more across Canada within the next three years.

Upon closer inspection, the Cora's success story can also be partially attributed to knowing the difference between the product or service they are "selling" and what their customer is really "buying.

Think about it.

Most of us don't really buy shovels, fertilizer or car washes. What we're really buying, in many cases, are holes in the ground, green grass, and a quiet way to show off. Think about it. People don't buy breath mints. What they really buy is social acceptance. Men don't buy diamond rings. What they really "buy" is the unforgettable look on her face.

Cora's franchisee Rick Nicholson understands this difference better than most.

His location in Dieppe, NB led the chain with 41% growth in 2007 and if you were to ask Rick how he does it, he would confirm success has very little to do with menu selection, portion control, location and other tangible factors normally associated with this cost-sensitive, margin-driven industry.

Deep down, Rick knows his customers aren't really buying the food on a plate.

He recognizes that what his diners are really buying is a chance to spend quality time with friends and family.

With that focus, Rick has translated Madame Tsouflidous vision and passion to the frontline, delivering what he calls "Rays of Human Sunshine".

He and his team do it through Canada's first-ever "Cora's Sunshine Club". There is a "Sunshine play list" with bouncy, fun-driven music that keeps the atmosphere cheery. Team members have their own "Sunshine" business cards and Facebook account. Local artists draw Cora-type caricatures of regular customers and top employees. The caricatures hang in the restaurant.

According to Rick, one of the easiest ways to spread "human sunshine" is through the simple power of recognition which naturally inspires team members to want to do the same for their customers. As you might expect, repeat business consistently exceeds industry average while turnover at Cora's Dieppe is well below what is considered standard in the food service sector.

Clearly, Cora's vision has had an impact that reaches far beyond her original Montreal snack bar. When it comes to understanding entrepreneurship, this lady offers a "been there, done that" perspective few can match. *"It was never really a question of wondering whether it was going to be easy or not: I just did it. Today I realize the more comfortable someone is in their job, the more difficult it will be for that person because of the sacrifices that will have to be made. That's what makes it* difficult to get in touch with our inner entrepreneur, that longing to be in control of our own life rather than being at someone else's mercy. I don't think it's harder today than it used to be, but the more comfortable we are, the more difficult it will be."

In 2004, Madame Tsouflidou was inducted into the Canadian Professional Sales Association's Hall of Fame and in 2005 received the Hall of Fame award from the Canadian Franchise Association. Her company has been named one of "Canada's 50 Best Managed Companies" and along the way Cora captured the "Femmes d'Affaires du Quebéc" (Quebec Business Women's) award for Entrepreneur of the year.

And her dream of becoming a writer?

"A few years ago a publisher asked me to write a book. This is my message: if you believe it, you can achieve it."

Upon reading her story, Rick was inspired to start working for himself and jumped into the trenches as a line cook for a year, before finally buying his own Cora's franchise. Passion, it would appear, can be contagious.

Cora's story not only serves as a reminder of the "turning lemons into lemonade" approach to life's challenges, but also recognizes the fact that life - by its very nature - is unfair to begin with. The consistent pattern from Cora's and other personal success stories seems to focus on how we respond to the unfairness surrounding us nearly every day. Undoubtedly, there were days when Cora had to say to herself, **"Gotta suck it up, buttercup"**.

Working with passion with what she had, and not worrying about she didn't have, Cora decided to do just that and "Get Cracking". Plugging into deeper, emotional needs of her customers, and creating a sense of belonging - as opposed to just serving bacon and eggs - has allowed her and the extended Cora's family to experience a sense of purpose rivalled by few.

Breakfast in Canada has never been the same since.

"You are the sunshine of my life, that's why I'll always stay around. You are the apple of my eye, forever you'll stay in my heart" **-STEVIE WONDER**

23
Brand in a Brilliant Disguise

Sitting and waiting in a McDonald's drive-thru, Brian was stuck in more ways than one.

It was 1989 and Brian had dropped out of his Vancouver-area high school.

One course short of graduation.

According to some of his teachers, he was also two bricks shy of a load with more than a few loose screws. Easily bored, Brian couldn't see the point learning about subjects he would never use in real life. He was different than most students. When a neighbourhood kid across the street set up a $2 car wash, Brian responded by copying the idea and charging $1.50.

Waiting in line that day for a cheeseburger and fries, listening to the Boss, Brian was struck by a vision.

Straight between his disbelieving eyes.

From that moment, Brian was ready to sweat it out in the streets of a runaway Canadian dream.

"I knew I needed to find a way to pay for college. In the drive-thru there was a beat-up pickup in front of me that said Mark's Hauling. I thought the hauling business was a great idea and with my last $700, I bought a truck and got started. I drove around town and when I saw someone with a pile of junk I knocked on their door and offered to take it away for a fee. That helped fund my college education. I actually dropped out one year before graduation because I was learning more from my business than from school. One year shy of a degree and here I am, a full-time JUNKMAN! My father, a liver transplant surgeon, was not impressed, to say the least."

From the moment his business was born to run, Brian was a risk-taker and a vision-maker. Able to see a brilliant future in a grungy disguise.

And do something about it.

Christening his new company as "The Rubbish Boys", Brian translated dreams and vision into action.

In two short years, the new Boss and his Boys were hauling trash to the tune of about $800,000 in annual revenues, with about a dozen employees serving the Vancouver and Victoria markets. Then one day, an entrepreneurial friend named Norm, suggested he pick up a business book.

The "E-Myth Revisited".

Brian retreated to Rathtrevor Beach on Vancouver Island and voraciously consumed its contents cover-to-cover.

Then he read it again.

And strapped his dreams across its engines.

Finishing a book is a rare accomplishment for a hyperactive dreamer like Brian, let alone reading one twice. But there was something in Michael Gerber's masterpiece that spoke volumes about his junk business - and where it would end up if he didn't do certain things.

The next day, 26-year old Brian marched into his weekly meeting with seven or eight other young entrepreneurs and dropped his copy of the E-Myth on the boardroom table.

His words exploded like a hand grenade tossed into a flower bed.

"This is, by far and without question, the best business book I've ever read"!

"THE BEST!!!"

Looking back, Brian says nothing has changed from what he learned on the beach that day and he still refers to E-Myth Revisited as his business "bible".

"I was blown away by the fact that nobody in this group of Young Entrepreneurs I was associated with had read the book or even heard of it. I told them that day it was going to have a great impact on the future of my business and theirs as well. More than anything, the E-Myth taught me to build your business like a franchise - even if you don't want to franchise it. Because franchising is a way to take best practices and recreate them in such a way that they easily become repeatable and scalable. And it applies to all aspects of the business; recruiting, training, marketing, operations, finance, etc."

This is interesting Brian ... tell us more.

"If you want to grow your business beyond being the person who does all of the day-to-day work, the E-Myth is the easiest way. It's about stepping back and taking a look at ways to build repeatable and profitable business systems that everyday people can operate. Thanks to what we learned from the book, we created a no-blame environment at 1-800-GOT-JUNK? with an entire team fanatically focused on fixing systems. That's because people don't fail - systems do. On a daily basis we huddle at our headquarters, the JUNKTION and identify the systems in our company that need fixing".

Michel Gerber has composed much more than just another business book.

To suggest otherwise would be like saying Springsteen cut just another record when he released *"Born in the USA"* or Spielberg shot just another movie with *"Saving Private Ryan"*. If you want to survive life in the business fast lane, without getting slaughtered financially, emotionally, or otherwise, RUN - don't walk and discover this gift for yourself. Gerber's masterpiece is the only book I heartily endorse with a money-back guarantee. Whether I am chatting with an entrepreneur one-on-one or addressing a business audience through the course of seminars and speaking engagements, the guarantee sounds something like this: *"You go spend 25 bucks on E-Myth Revisited and if you don't see the value in what Gerber is saying, and the gift he is sharing, I'll buy the book back from you - no questions asked. And just so you know, I don't make a nickel off it - I just believe in the book that much".*

Why does Gerber's message matter so much?

It's about having a clear understanding of business fundamentals that challenge traditional beliefs about owning and operating a business.

Michael Gerber has succeeded in packaging these fundamentals better than anyone else; sharing his ideas in the form of a story where you, the entrepreneur, become the main character. Essentially you wind up reading about yourself and how your business movie will end. Here are just a few of the pearls you'll find buried in the pages of this entrepreneurial epic.

- **E-Myth:** The "entrepreneurial myth" that most people who start small businesses are entrepreneurs. Most just start a business as a place to go to work.
- **The Fatal Assumption:** That an individual who understands the technical work of a business can automatically know how to own and operate a business that does technical work.
- **Clarity:** The difference between working "on" your business not "in" it. The difference between owning the business and having it own you.
- **Purpose:** Sole function of a business is to create and keep customers.

Entrepreneurship represents a relatively new field of professional education with about a 40-year history, but what key dimensions affect the relationship between you as the lead actor, the process and the results? If you are already in business or hunger to start your own, Michael Gerber forces you to ask yourself - the owner of that business - some tough questions about those relationships. Not the types of questions that your banker, friend, relative or customer will ask, but rather questions that require a decision from the owner. Ignorance of the Laws of the Business Universe is no excuse. Part and parcel of success is having clarity on why you are even heading to this mountain in the first place.

As Gerber points out *"We're born to climb our metaphorical mountain. Sadly, out of the 6 billion among us, the majority will settle and stay in the valley, never getting on the hill. Eating, sleeping, feeding and creating new beings, most who also stay in the valley. Every once in a while we look up and say "one day, one day ..." but we worry because no one who goes up there ever comes back. But once you've lived on the mountain, there is no way you can go return to the valley because you'll want to stay with all the crazy people enjoying the view from this mountain; the one with an infinite peak because there is no top to it".*

Having had his eyes and imagination opened with E-Myth thinking, Brian realized he needed to develop a clear vision. While sitting on the dock at his parents' summer cottage on Bowen

Island, British Columbia, he scribbled his "painted picture". Two pages outlining the company's future mansion of glory. He also established a lofty goal: In five years, he wanted the 1-800-GOT-JUNK? brand to be found in all 30 U.S. and Canadian cities larger than Vancouver. As Brian explains," I wanted to create the 'FedEx' of junk removal".

Franchise Number One was launched in 1999 in Toronto.

The 5-year goal was achieved 16 days ahead of schedule.

Brian Scudamore's recipe for business and branding success has been simple.

Take a fragmented, mom-and-pop business model and give it a branding makeover with clean shiny trucks that act as mobile billboards, uniformed drivers, on-time service and up-front rates. Mix in a hip culture of cool that is young, fun and completely focused on healthy, profitable growth. Ensure a foundation for the future by retaining 100% ownership and bootstrapping the business solely out of cash flow.

Although 1-800-GOT-JUNK? is a simple business, it could not have enjoyed rapid growth without technology-driven systems. All calls come into a central 1-800-GOT-JUNK? call centre where they do all the booking and dispatch for their franchise partners. Franchise partners then assess their real-time reports, schedules, customer info, etc., on JUNKNET, their corporate intranet. This allows franchise partners to get into business quickly, and to focus solely on growth — working on the business as opposed to working in the business.

So Brian ... why aren't more entrepreneurs rushing out, grabbing a copy of E-Myth Revisited and applying its principles?

"I think it comes down to the difference between being a doer or a thinker. Especially in the start-up phase, a business owner has to be a hard-core doer - but eventually, you've got to get other people around you to do the doing. Otherwise, you need to question if you are truly serious about building a business. Essentially you need to be able to systematize your business to the point where you can take ten weeks vacation and not have to check in".

1-800-GOT-JUNK? is now established in every major city in North America with a population exceeding one million people. That translates into more than a thousand trucks, serving more than 250 locations, generating more than $100 million in revenue. Upwards of a thousand people now make a living through Brian's brand, 25 of which have become millionaires.

"With this company, I made the future happen in my mind. Once I became very centred in that picture, it was clear we would get there. We believe 100 percent that we will get to a billion in total sales. Any entrepreneur, or any leader, for that matter—in religion, in athletics— needs a clear vision."

Business is dazzling in its richness, variation and depth. A palette far broader than most people realize. To see commerce as nothing more than broad brushstrokes consisting of the reward is to miss seeing the brilliant nuances and infinite number of dramatic events that produces profit or loss. Owning a business is more than just a vehicle to make money. It's a way to become who you are. It will both test your character and reveal it. When F.W. Woolworth opened his very first store, a competitor across the street hung out a sign that read "Doing business in this same spot for over 50 years" The next day Woolworth hung out his own sign saying "Established a week ago. No old stock"

If a business is to grow, you have to own it – the daily tasks, Joe jobs and grunt labour. Your beginning will determine all that follows. And in the beginning, survival is more important than success. Your chance of survival grows exponentially by adopting E-Myth principles that help you stay on the field, play the game and learn the rules as you grow. The critical ingredient is getting off your butt and doing something. A lot of people have ideas, but few decide to do something about them now. Not tomorrow or next week, but today. True entrepreneurs are doers. Not dreamers.

What kind of business do you want for yourself? Are you ready to discover the bedrock principles to shape your relationship with that business? Will you see the wisdom in applying what Michael Gerber, Brian Scudamore and thousands of other successful entrepreneurs want to share with you?

The 1-800-GOT-JUNK? story has been told on Oprah and Dr. Phil, written about in USA Today, The New York Times, Wall Street Journal, and the Associated Press and has attracted recognition with numerous business and humanitarian awards including, the Fortune Small Business: Best Boss Award, Entrepreneur Magazine's: Franchise 500, and The Best Company To Work for award by BC Business Magazine.

But Brian would be the first to tell you that it was power of another story that allowed 1-800-GOT-JUNK? to break out of a trap that leaves many business highways jammed with broken heroes on a last chance power drive.

A story that will steady the madness in your entrepreneurial soul.

And guide you to that place in the sun where you want your business to go.

"When it comes to luck, you make your own."
-BRUCE SPRINGSTEEN

24
Messing with Words

Waiting for a flight several years ago at Dallas-Fort Worth International, I wandered into an airport souvenir shop. With time to kill and a few dollars to burn, it wasn't long before the eyes of Texas were staring back at me in the form of a coffee cup.

The message was loud and clear.

"Don't Mess with Texas"

I was taken aback by the spirit of bravado. Was this some kind of threat? The words seemed to pack their own kind of heat, with a lazy drawl dripping from the lip of that menacing mug. As the message sunk in, I was under the immediate impression that there were dire consequences in store for any hombre foolish enough to cross any native of America's 28th state.

Weeks later, I discovered the real story.

And further evidence of the behaviour-shaping power of words.

In 1985 the state of Texas had a serious problem with litter, spending $25 million a year on cleanup. Costs were rising at about 15% annually until December of that year, when a bumper sticker bearing the words "Don't Mess With Texas" began appearing on pickup trucks across the Lone Star State.

There was no explanation.

Just four words with a small red, white, and blue Texas flag.

Fast-forward more than 20 years to today and the longest-running public service campaign in Texas is also the most successful anti-litter campaign in history, reducing litter on highways by an astonishing 72 percent. The media campaign premiered January 1, 1986 with a television advertisement at the 50th annual Cotton Bowl featuring blues legend, Stevie Ray Vaughn.

Since then, numerous musicians, athletes, celebrities and other famous Texans have appeared in "Don't Mess with Texas" radio and television ads, including Warren Moon, Jerry Jeff Walker, Willie Nelson, George Foreman, and LeAnn Rimes.

More than its immediate success at reducing litter, however, the slogan also became a Texas cultural icon and the slogan adopted for general use. "Don't Mess with Texas" has also earned a spot among the best ever advertising slogans, with a plaque on the Madison Avenue Walk of Fame and a plaque in the Advertising Hall of Fame.

The words we choose to describe our businesses, our brands and how behaviour can subsequently be influenced can have gi-normous repercussions - provided they are chosen wisely and handled with care. Whenever we speak or write, our words become vehicles that transport meaning – and positive or negative energy - to others. The words may be in the form of an advertising message, a work-related memo, or a love letter, but each word brings with it emotional baggage and power to educate, inform or persuade.

Some of us know this instinctively.

Others arrive at this understanding slowly.

This blinding grasp of the obvious became vividly apparent to me in March of 2000. I was travelling on a five-hour hockey road trip to Cape Breton, Nova Scotia. Sitting at the back of the Tim Hortons All-Stars bus, Robbie Forbes handed over a copy of *Secret Formulas of the Wizard of Ads*. For the next several hours, I eagerly consumed it. Cover to cover. I was

propelled in no small part by the captivating effect of Chapter 1 where author Roy H. Williams articulates how words are electric and should be chosen for the emotional voltage they carry. To paraphrase the Wizard:

"Monumental events explode with energetic words, and great leaders are remembered for the things they say. While a grand idea may carry the seeds of change, it takes powerful words to launch the idea skyward.

Words are electric, and should be chosen for the emotional voltage they carry. Weak and predictable words cause grand ideas to appear so dull that they fade into the darkness of oblivion. But powerful words, staggered in unusual combinations, brightly illuminate the mind.

Words start wars and end them, create love and choke it, bring us to laughter, joy and tears. Words cause men and women to willingly risk their lives, their fortunes, their sacred honor. Our world as we know it, revolves on the power of words"

Few understand the energy of the perfect word better than political wordsmith extraordinaire Frank Luntz.

The author of *Words that Work,* Luntz is responsible for classic phrases as "war on terror," "death tax," "energy exploration," "climate change" and "healthy-forests initiative". These are the phrases formerly known as "foreign war", "estate tax", "oil-drilling", "global warming" and "clear cutting". According to Luntz, "It's not what you say. It's what people hear". Cynics are quick to dismiss his strategies as ways to skew the truth and spread "political bullshit" - but Luntz, could respond to the criticism by justifying his craft as "vital excremental resources".

There is no denying it. Words create the fabric of our reality.

They can cloak wonderful ideas with weak-kneed clichés, hindering the potential to alchemize these thoughts and turn branding straw into gold. Or, they can be like seeds lying dormant, waiting for the perfect moment to sprout and explode with emotional intensity. Such was the case in 1947, when a young copywriter struggled to find the right words to solve her client's problem. The client, a mining company, wanted to sell colourless stones with almost zero practical use. Sure, you could grind them up and put them on drill bits, but Frances Gerety, working on a deadline and losing sleep, wondered how she could connect romance, essentially worthless crystals, and human desire, in a way which would move these rocks. As Gerety remembers it, "Dog tired, I put my head down and said, 'Please God, send me a line'."

Legend has it that after a restless, dream-filled sleep, Frances was awakened, consumed with a single thought. Within three years, 80 per cent of American engagements were starting with a diamond ring - thanks to the four words that came to Frances in her sleep. In the year 2000, Advertising Age magazine named her epiphany, "A Diamond Is Forever", from the mining company known as De Beers, the best advertising slogan of the twentieth century.

Other jewels include:

Just do it
Tastes great, less filling
We try harder
Good to the last drop
Breakfast of champions
Where's the beef?
Don't leave home without it
Nothing sucks like an Electrolux

Wordsmithing was a crucial talent required for the print and radio heydays of advertising. The craft suffered when TV went big in the 60's. But in the 21st century Digital Age - where content is king - skilful, elegant phraseology is once again holding court.

What words are energizing your brand?

Are they direct? Unexpected? Believable?

Or will readers of your website and marketing materials discover hollow, polite, or sluggish words? Worse, do the people who work with your organization pepper prospects and customers with self-promoting hype, pomposity and puffery? Are you open to possibilities that lie within your grasp by using sparkling, pristine words to electrify and illuminate your brand?

Be clear, not clever. Employ words that will perform some heavy lifting in answering a prospect's question "Why you, not somebody else?" before it even escapes her lips.

The careful choice of four simple words inspired millions of Texans to keep 261,797 square miles free of trash.

And millions more worldwide to fall head over heels in a crystallized commitment to eternal love.

Have you chosen precise, unpredictable, priceless words to unleash the passion, energy and spirit of your brand?

"You can go to hell ... and I'll go to Texas"
-DAVY CROCKETT

25
Something Different

What would inspire someone to compose a "Bucket List" in their early thirties, and then take two years off from the "real world" to complete it?

Has there been a defining moment in your life when you were tempted to scream "enough" and start living life to the beat of your own bongo? Deep down, isn't that one of your fantasies? To be able to say "To hell with chasing cheese as just another rodent in this race. I'm going to saunter through life at my own pace; do exactly what I want and do it when I am damn well good and ready".

In Cheryl's case, her "list" began forming each time she heard her father saying for the thousandth-and-one time "Can't wait until I retire … then I'm going to do the things I want to do". George's list was filled with hiking adventures, RV excursions, European vacations and much, much more, until one day, George retired from his job at a Minnesota munitions plant.

Six months later George was diagnosed with lung cancer. Within three months he passed away.

Gone at age 62.

Wiping back tears of grief, Cheryl made a promise to herself, vowing, "I'm not ever going to wait to retire before I start living. Life happens now".

First, she resigned from her decade-long position as public relations director for a company building resorts in Mexico. Then, over the next 24 months, the native of Anoka, Minnesota crossed off most of the items from her own "bucket list".

Learned to speak Spanish by living with a Mexican family in a small village north of Mexico City.

Learned to sail after volunteering to work as third person on a crew with two strangers. Did a 900 nautical mile adventure from Cancun to Galveston, TX on a 27-foot schooner.

- Learned to experience "oneness" by living in peace and tranquillity for several weeks at a yoga ashram outside of San Francisco.
- Took college classes for the sheer joy of learning. Cheryl studied sociology and philosophy. Not as part of a degree program but because she craved a deeper knowledge of those subjects.
- Learned how to negotiate low-cost travel with jaunts to France, Germany, Spain, Switzerland, Austria, Italy, England, Belgium, the West Indies, Belize, and about 42 of the United States of America.

-
- And perhaps, most importantly, Cheryl learned how to strike up meaningful conversations. In bus depots and sidewalk cafés. On front porches and subway platforms. She learned how to really listen to real people and their funny, sad, ordinary, inspiring, mundane, painful and joyful stories. She listened without distraction. After all Cheryl didn't have to be somewhere else. She had no meetings to get ready for, no career agenda that needed advancing.

She just listened.

Until it was time to go.

Back home and busted financially and living with Mom, but, richer and wiser for the experience, Cheryl decided it was time for something different. So that's what she named her new store. Owning her own business was the only thing that made sense since she figured "The only person who would hire me was myself. I had been out on my own for too long and besides, I didn't want to wear pantyhose or high heels ever again".

In a town of 17,000 souls, with Anoka's downtown filled with "For Lease" signs, Cheryl launched *Something Different*, out of a 250-square foot hole in the wall, selling giftware and decorative accessories you wouldn't find through major retailers. *"Something Different"* blossomed with legendary tales of service that touched hearts and created customers for life.

145

The Vandermeer sisters discovered it for themselves when they rushed in frantically one Sunday afternoon. They were already late for a bridal shower - being held 75 miles away. And there was a snowstorm on. Calmly, Cheryl helped the ladies find an appropriate gift, wrapping it in such exquisite fashion that was guaranteed to draw admiring "ooohs" and "aaahs". Hurrying out to their car and bracing themselves for the trip, the sisters were shocked when Cheryl followed them out, placed a pocket angel in each of their hands and wished them safe travels.

The sisters become lifetime customers.

The way Cheryl explains it, "We never know what happens when we do little insignificant ways to show we care. The smallest of acts can actually make a significant difference".

In the spring of the year 2000, Cheryl would discover the truth of her own words, when the phone rang one Monday morning at her home in Key Largo, Florida.

A former boyfriend was on the line, from 1800 miles away.

Within moments Cheryl learned that Shaun's daughter had been placed in an institution to protect herself - a 16-year old dealing with personal demons so dark they had pushed her to a dangerous edge.

Twice.

And even though the relationship with Shaun had ended, Cheryl had kept in touch with his daughter and through the course of this emotional phone call learned what was at stake. "She is in the state hospital and you can't visit because you are not family, but you're the only person we think who can get through to her. She won't listen to anyone else".

Cheryl was lost for words.

"All I could think about was this beautiful girl with so much promise, so much going for her, locked up in this grey room with four walls closing in and bars on the window"

Thanking Shaun for the call, she hung up.

And went to work.

Recovering from her shock, Cheryl wasted no time in sending Madison messages of comfort. Cards and notes sent via snail mail three or four times a week. Grasping for something, anything, to somehow find the right things to say to connect with a troubled teenager trying to escape a living hell.

About six weeks later, in the still of the night, Cheryl roared awake at about 4 a.m. with a flash of inspiration that would not be silenced. She would create something that Madison would have on her nightstand - a permanent reminder of how much she was loved. She was going to create a unique, one-on-one book containing three, unconditional promises to Madison.

"My mind was racing, hands trembling, the ink just poured on to 2x4 note cards as though it flowed from another source. I just filled those cards with all the things I wished somebody would have said to me when I was 16 years old and doubting my own magnificence. It was in those moments I could picture a book that would act as a living entity and be able to reach out as if to hold Madison's hand. I wanted her to know she could call at any time, at any hour, and I would be there for her. At the very beginning of her book I made a place to write my phone number so she knew I was serious. And right beside the phone number I wrote about my promise to listen - really listen - whenever that call came through. Finally, I promised to listen without judging".

"Once I started sharing my story about Maddy, people started sharing their own heartbreaking stories and kept asking for a similar book for their son, daughter, niece, nephew or what have you. It's like the world was telling me to help others who were searching for a way in which they could reach out to someone in need. It was enlightening to me that thousands of Maddys were out there".

Soon after "Eat Your Peas for Young Adults" was published; people began to ask Karpen if she had the same promise for full-grown adults. As she puts it, "I realized it isn't just young people who need to be reminded how truly special they are. We all do".

What began as a one-person crusade to help restore a teenager's faith in herself, is now sprouting hope and inspiration throughout North America and other parts of the world. Lovingly illustrated by Sandy Fougner, there are 21 "Eat Your Peas" publications currently available, with promises intended for each member of the family as well as in-laws, new moms, girlfriends, holidays, birthdays, tough times and more.

Words of gratitude flow into Cheryl's inbox daily.

I have read many spiritual, religious and grievance books. None have come close to the book I was given by a friend at Alanon called "Eat Your Peas for Tough Times". I want to read it out loud at the meeting, but we cannot read non-approved Alanon literature. I will however, pass it on to everyone I know who can use some help during those tough times. I don't like to complain, but if I know there is friend who will listen sometimes, I will definitely reach out. I am broken in pieces. Thank you for taking the time to touch people like me with your words of wisdom. Your book is a blessing from God.

I received my first Peas book under the Christmas tree a few years ago. The book was "Eat Your Peas for Teens" and it was from my mother; this has been my very favourite book that ever since. Over the last few years I have paged through the book literally hundreds of times and showed all of my friends my most treasured book. Really appreciate the love and hard work that goes into the "Eat Your Peas" collection. I now know what I can get every single person on my Christmas list!!

I have been helping people through some of the roughest spots in their lives and wanted to find a new way to tell them that they are important and special to somebody in the world. I also always inform them of how I will always be there for them but I needed a new way of getting this message across. "Eat Your Peas" books are the answer I've been praying for, so I thank God everyday for Cheryl's idea!

And as for the girl who inspired the series, Maddy not only went on to make a full and complete recovery, she wound up graduating the next spring with a university degree in Environmental Science.

Cheryl embodies an ideal that many talk about but rarely act on. As Mother Teresa was once quoted as saying, *"If we want a love message to be heard, it has got to be sent out. To keep a lamp burning, we have to keep putting oil in it. Do not wait for leaders; do it alone, person to person".*

No love would have been sent had Cheryl not listened to the sound of her own voice and lit her own fire. She made a decision not to procrastinate. She did what mattered most. She refused to postpone life until the day when all the bills were paid and there was lots of free time.

Cheryl Karpen's publishing company, based in Anoka, Minnesota, is selling more than 10,000 books that touch hearts and souls each month. And if you were wondering about the title, Cheryl says she borrowed it from her mother's refrain often heard around the family dinner table.

"Eat your peas. They're good for you".

How do you define success? When was the last time you checked your list?

Has your typical day become an endurance test of what you can tolerate? Has life been whispering to? Suggesting you do things differently? Nudging you to make use of your talents and abilities? What are your greatest strengths and how are you leveraging them? Are there seemingly insignificant ways to serve others that might make a significant difference"?

Is it time for you to do something different?

""But I can say that life is good to me. Has been and is good. So I think my task is to be good to it. So how do you be good to life? You live it." **-MORGAN FREEMAN**

26
Who's Teaching Who

The Risky Business of Education

What wisdom would you share, if you were invited to speak before a class of so-called, "at-risk" teenagers? You know - the 16 and 17-year olds who have fallen through the wide cracks that exist in any school system. Young adults, who are struggling to:

a) Keep up with their with grades
b) Fit in and play nice with others
c) Find out who they really are
d) Stay away from temptation and trouble
e) All of the above.

I'm not sure if I'm the best person to speak on any subject involving "at-risk" youth, as I can't help but wonder if there may be a flaw with the fundamental starting point in this exercise.

Define "At-Risk". According to whom?

What if these kids are really in a state of "At-Opportunity"?

The pursuit of any endeavour of consequence entails a greater appetite for risk and as such lies the potential for greater reward. Maybe being labelled "at-risk" in the W.F.O.* Digital Age isn't such a bad thing after all.

Might depend on how you look at it.

But, let's get back to the invitation to speak.

My initial response is that I am a lousy choice for this gig. Deep down, I know with unbending certainty I have not travelled any of the same roads as these teens. I was the kind of kid who did okay in school, graduated on time, made friends easily, avoided the "bad" crowd and only got into minimal, harmless amounts of trouble. Don't get me wrong, our family was as dysfunctional as the next, but the record shows I did have two parents who worked, paid their bills, stayed together and after grabbing my high school diploma helped me enrol in a Toronto college to launch a career in broadcasting.

But the decades-plus friend who is inviting me to speak to these "at-risk" kids believes I have something of value to share.

Even if I don't quite believe it myself.

"OK, Debbie, I'll do it".

The appointed day arrives. The second I walk into class, the anticipated differences were clear. We have as much in common as a New York night and a Maritime morning. They are younger; I am part of what's politely being called an "older demographic". They're clad in jeans and t-shirts; I'm decked out in business casual. Most of them exude street cred cool with little or no effort. I'm still struggling in that department.

Confession. I have yet to learn how to text message another living human.

"This is going to be hard ... harder than I thought ... How do I make a connection with these kids? ... How do I inspire them in some authentic way that might make a difference in how they see the world and themselves in it? OK, Einstein, anytime now, what genius brainwave can you come up with?"

That's it!

After the initial introductions and going around the room to put names to the 24 faces, I thought if there was any wisdom to be discovered on this day, it could only come from them. In other words, they were no different than many of the larger, corporate groups I am regularly invited to speak to. Like adult-learners, they didn't need yet another know-it-all Moses coming down from the mountain tops, preaching a sermon on success.

The answers were already inside them. Just needed to be extracted.

Here is the question that was asked:

"What would be the common traits, characteristics or accomplishments shared by Einstein and Eminem?

Come again?

"You heard me, what is the same or similar about Einstein and Eminem? And I'm expecting a different answer from each of you. No one can pass on this question and I will tell you up front, it's much easier to go first, since the answers will be tougher to come up with as we work our way around the class and get

towards the end of the room"

This question is greeted with stony silence.

Tension slowly fills the room.

Two-dozen borderline high school dropouts are gradually realizing this will not be an easy task to accomplish, demanding 24 original answers from start to finish.

With anxious hesitation, one student begins.

Then another.

After a few hiccups along the way, the task has been completed. A flip chart bears testament to 24 original answers to the question.

1. Both names start with the letter "E".
2. Both are men.
3. Both are smart.
4. Both changed lives.
5. Both did drugs.
6. Both had hard childhoods.
7. Both were wrong at times.
8. Both were doubted.
9. Both were persecuted, judged and put down.
10. Both are tops in their profession.
11. Both are famous.
12. Both are committed.
13. Both inspired people.
14. Both worked their way to the top.
15. Both had two "E's" in each of their names.
16. Both are smart.
17. Both are legends.
18. Both were ahead of their time.
19. Both were subjects of discussion.
20. Both were idealists.
21. Both were a little weird.
22. Both changed lives.
23. Both had dreams and created their own path.
24. Neither completed high school.

I learned something more important than my audience that day.

Collectively, this "at-risk" crowd appeared more than satisfied with what they had accomplished while I realized the roles had suddenly reversed in terms of who was teaching whom. As the final answer went up on the chart, I couldn't help but think:

"Excellence has nothing to do with how, or where, you begin. It's where you end up. It's not how you start, its how you finish"

I was also left with the opinion that these kids may be racing ahead of what any educational system could provide them, in terms of being able to harness latent talents and inner greatness. But school systems weren't built that way to begin. Children are herded into a factory model with batches called grades, effectively excluding outsiders who don't quite "fit in".

But the fact remains that there is a glaring difference between what is required for academic success: *Primarily solitary study, few distractions, single subject concentration and loads of written work*

vs.

What is essential for business success: *Working in teams, constant distractions, multi-tasking, and speaking skills.*

As a result, most 21st century education systems are:

Sadly,
Totally,
Absolutely,
Terribly,
Unequivocally,
Shamefully,

and ...

Quite,
Unprepared,
Organizationally ...

... to deal with cataclysmic forces of technological, societal, environmental, political, organizational and economic change playing havoc with the "real world" our kids are being prepared for.

There is, however, at least one uncommonly remarkable voice willing to stand up and be counted. And, as a PhD, his message has a chance of being heard, and hopefully, help those educators in lofty positions who make vital decisions, see their way out of this education wilderness.

Sir Ken Robinson is an internationally recognized leader in the development of creativity, innovation and human resources. He has worked with governments in Europe and Asia, international agencies, Fortune 500 companies, national and state education systems, non-profit corporations and some of the world's leading cultural organizations. In 1998 Robinson was invited by the UK Government to establish and lead a national commission on creativity, education and the economy.

Leading business people, scientists, artists and educators all weighed in and *The Robinson Report* was published to huge acclaim. The London Times said: 'This report raises some of the most important issues facing business in the 21st century. It should have every CEO and human resources director thumping the table and demanding action'.

"Employers are already saying a degree is not enough, and that graduates do not have the qualities they are looking for; the ability to communicate, work in teams, adapt to change, to innovate and be creative. This is not surprising ... the traditional academic curriculum is not designed to promote creativity. Complaining that the system does not produce creative people is like complaining that a car doesn't fly ... it was never intended to. The stark message is that the answer to the future is not simply to increase the amount of education, but to educate people differently." **-SIR KEN ROBINSON PhD**

How much longer can we afford the human, emotional and financial costs incurred by archaic, top-down, command-and-control instruction that tends to eradicate original, inventive thought? Can any company or nation compete on the global stage with a work force supplied by left-brain (nuts & bolts) dominant education systems that stunt right-brain (a few loose screws) creativity?

In terms of acquiring real wisdom, deep reservoirs of talent exist everywhere, provided you will only we stop and listen long and hard enough.

Who do you think is really at risk when it comes to education?

"The truth is you don't know what is going to happen tomorrow. Life is a crazy ride, and nothing is guaranteed." **-EMINEM**

NOTE: Marshall Bruce Mathers III, also known as "Slim Shady" and his primary nom de plume, "Eminem", is an Academy Award winning and Grammy Award winning rapper/actor who has sold over seventy million albums worldwide. He has collaborated with various artists such as Dr. Dre, 50-Cent, Kid Rock, Missy Elliott, Jay-Z, Notorious B.I.G., Jadakiss and others.

Six months after he was born, Marshall's father disappeared.

As a kid, Marshall moved a lot, repeated the ninth grade three times and dropped out of high school at 17. He has attempted suicide, been sued for $10 million dollars by his birth mother, and is twice-divorced from the mother of his daughter Hailie Jade. He has been praised for having "verbal energy", high quality of lyricism and earned notoriety for controversial lyrical themes, alleged to glorify violence, misogyny and homophobia.

His music kicks serious ass.

Meanwhile, Albert Einstein received the 1921 Nobel Prize in Physics for his services to Theoretical Physics, and especially for his discovery of the law of the Photoelectric Effect. His vast contributions to our planet include his Theory of Relativity and his discovery that energy and mass are equivalent and transmutable. ($E=MC^2$).

In 1999, Albert was named "Person of the Century" by TIME Magazine.

In his early teens, Einstein clashed with authorities and resented the regimen of school. He later wrote that the spirit of learning and creative thought were lost in strict rote learning. At 16 he dropped out, convincing the school to let him go by using a doctor's note. Rather than complete high school, Albert applied directly to Swiss Federal Institute of Technology in Zurich. Without a diploma, he was required to take an entrance examination, which he did not pass, although he got exceptional marks in mathematics and physics.

Eventually, Albert would rock our world.

As would Marshall.

"I, at any rate, am convinced that God does not throw dice." **-ALBERT EINSTEIN**

Side Four

"I always believed in the music we did and that's why it was uncompromising"

-JIMMY PAGE

27
Virtuoso of Vision

You may be familiar with the expression "Our attitude almost always determines our altitude". But just how far can that take you or any organization you may be a part of?

Buckle up.

Stow away the tray table. Get ready to fly around the world and back.

The year is 2002. Fourteen-year old Erika approaches the mail box at her suburban home in Moncton, NB with mixed emotions of fear, anxiety and anticipation. Twice previously she has been rejected in her attempts to earn a spot as a violinist with the New Brunswick Youth Orchestra. Erika has been hoping and praying for weeks that "third time lucky" will do the trick.

She picks up the envelope bearing the NBYO logo. Slowly she tears it open.

Her face radiates unspeakable joy. Whew! Waves of relief and excitement swell in a crescendo. A happy dance ensues.

Several weeks later, Erika and her dad drive to the first rehearsal weekend in nearby St. Martins. Easy-going Ken chats with other proud parents of these musical prodigies and before too long winds up in a conversation with the orchestra's president, Barbara Clarke. Informal chit-chat soon turns to another letter, one that NBYO had recently received, postmarked "Carnegie Hall".

Casually, Barbara mentions that thanks to a recommendation from an anonymous patron, Carnegie Hall was extending an invitation for this otherwise obscure ensemble of New Brunswick teenagers to perform on what is regarded as the stage of stages. The Mecca of classical music.

"There's no way we can do this. We've always struggled just to stay afloat financially and as a parent-supported orchestra,

the funds just aren't there to make this sort of thing happen". Many of the parents nod and agree.

Listening intently, Erika's dad - who is just getting his feet wet in his first day on the job as an NBYO parent - chimes in: *"How can we not say yes?"*

Ken's observation is greeted with stunned silence.

Moments pass before someone stammers, *"Well, if we can find the money ..."*

And it is in fleeting moments like these that visionaries like Ken MacLeod emerge to change the world you and I live in. Wikipedia defines a visionary as one who experiences a vision that involves seeing into the future - someone able to simply imagine that which does not yet exist - but that might some day. Examples of great visionaries include Buckminster Fuller in architecture and design, Steve Jobs in technology and, before the turn of the last century, industrialist Andrew Carnegie. An immigrant son of poor Scottish farmers, the steel tycoon/philanthropist ended up donating $350,000,000 to charity, helping build 2,500 libraries as well as Carnegie Mellon University and the world-famous Hall that bears his name in midtown Manhattan.

"I'm sure if we started asking, there are others who would pitch in and help", suggested Ken. With his background in academia, government and charitable work, Ken offered to take the ball and run with it. He started asking people he knew that would care enough to see New Brunswick kids shine in a musical heaven where legendary artists such as George Gershwin, Benny Goodman, Isaac Stern, Ella Fitzgerald, Duke Ellington, and a hip English quartet called The Beatles once performed.

The first phone call went to his marketing buddy David Hawkins who asked *"How can I help ..."*

Next, Ken reached President Larry Nelson of Lounsbury Company who piped up, *"We have to do this".*

Others followed suit.

Margaret McCain of Maple Leaf Foods.

Bernard and Monique Imbeault of Pizza Delight fame.

Before long Ken's fundraising efforts had generated $240,000, exceeding the original goal for the New York excursion by more than $45,000. He had acquired corporate sponsorships and support from other NBYO networks, and the kids themselves had held fund-raisers. $240,000 - from an orchestra that was used to operating on an annual budget of $30,000 with no staff support and parental volunteers managing the program.

But raising money wasn't the only challenge.

Other details included preparing the kids to play with proficiency at this level. Detailed logistics and planning were also required to move a small army of musicians and instruments and pull that off within the context of a post 9-11 environment. Parents had legitimate concerns about crossing the border, as well as personal safety issues once they had arrived in a shaken New York City. A city still reeling in shock and cleaning up from the terrorist attacks on the World Trade Center.

Under the guidance of conductor James Mark, a team of 70 New Brunswick classically-trained musicians between the ages of 12 and 22 experienced the thrill of a lifetime the first time they walked on stage for a dress rehearsal.

Jaws dropped and the magnitude of the moment started settling in as Mark and his charges suddenly understood what Stern himself had once remarked, *"The hall itself is an instrument"*, referring to the way the sound quality complements any artist's music. Acoustics so pristine they are breathtaking.

On June 29, 2003, the New Brunswick Youth Orchestra earned a thunderous and immediate standing ovation at Carnegie Hall as Ken and other proud parents celebrated this most unlikely of accomplishments. And it was in that moment that Ken couldn't help but recall his comment to the NBYO Board in October of 2002 that an appearance at Carnegie Hall would do more to advance the work of the orchestra than almost anything that had been done previously.

How prophetic.

But hey, that's what Visionary Virtuosos do.

They can see what's going to happen and then help make it happen. And in the case of the New Brunswick Youth Orchestra, Ken's vision, coupled with the capacity of a dedicated team to share the workload, has allowed young musicians from a small, out-of-the-way province achieve a level of success otherwise unimaginable.

The Carnegie Hall appearance was followed by a CD recording, *"Premiere"*, and a nationally televised CBC documentary, Practice, Practice, Practice. In 2005 the orchestra appeared in Parma, Italy, where they studied with world-class musicians and performed and recorded at the Auditorium Paganini. The orchestra's work was captured on their second CD, titled *"Virtuoso Italia"*. In 2007, it was off to China and a tour that included performances at the Forbidden City Concert Hall, Great Hall of the People and the Arts Centre of Hebei Province, as well as working with professional musicians from the Beijing Symphony and China Philharmonic orchestras. That experience was preserved with a third CD, titled "Forbidden City Tour", a disc that allowed NBYO to take home a 2008 East Coast Music Awards award for Classical Recording of the Year.

And to think a simple question from the new dad on the block started it all.

"How can we not say yes?"

The success of any endeavour you are involved in can only ever grow to the size and scope of its vision. Often overused, dismissed, and rarely understood, vision is vital if you hope to build anything greater than one's self. The common characteristic among visionaries is their ability to accurately assess the impact of decisions made today and how they will affect what transpires years, even decades down the road.

In other words, true visionaries possess unusually long time horizons as opposed to the average person who thinks ahead by exactly one paycheque. Hey wait a minute - is that part of the connection between attitude and altitude?

Ken MacLeod is a great example of a Visionary Virtuoso – applying principles similar to the ones that Fuller, Jobs, and Carnegie would employ to spot opportunities on distant horizons and take specific steps to get there. Visionary Virtuosos are both intuitive and pragmatic with a creative side that focuses on the "big picture" without getting lost in the seductive symphony of blue-sky discussions. These are the kind of people who make things happen – and often do.

Ken can't play an instrument to save his soul - but a different strain of music from his heart helped energize the New Brunswick Youth Orchestra brand, allowing it to appear in some the world's

161

top venues. The orchestra that once had difficulty attracting enough members to fill its required seats is now very much in demand and the subject of global, national and regional media attention.

Buckminster Fuller didn't require a majority vote to move forward with plans to construct the geodesic dome. Steve Jobs would not permit any excuses or delays to prevent the launch of the MacIntosh computer. Andrew Carnegie knew people would need those libraries and facilities someday. But at some point, each, in their own way, would have asked questions that sounded like:

"How can we not say yes?"

Visionaries like Ken MacLeod, who ask those types of questions, have the courage to put their heart on the line for something they believe in. In their book, *The Leader's Voice*, authors Clarke and Crossland argue that, *"Vision is a love affair with an idea"*.

How about you?

Is there an idea that you could have a love affair with?

Can you picture how a love affair that begins at your local or regional level can be accelerated and elevated through the sheer power of attitude and vision? Or do you really believe that a dynamic, compelling, all-encompassing vision ever comes to fruition by waiting around for what committees or consultants have to say?

Only you can decide whether the need for a majority vote, an excuse or fear is keeping you from fulfilling a vision you are madly in love with.

To what extent has your altitude been determined by your attitude and the way you envision potential opportunity? Have you fallen into the habit of thinking, "There's no way we can pull that off" or is there something happening right now where you want to exclaim, *"How can we not say yes?"*

Could you be ready to reach for higher notes?

It's never too late hum a new tune or sing a different song.

""Aim for the highest"   **-ANDREW CARNEGIE**

28
Wine, Winning, and Song

Being Bland IS: Safe.

Being Bland IS: Politically correct.

Being Bland MEANS: You won't get laughed at, second-guessed or criticized.

Being Bland TURNS: Your brand into the equivalent of the "Charlie Brown Teacher" reading 838 bullet points off 79 PowerPoint slides while 127 sets of eyeballs glaze over. "*Stab me in the eye with a dinner fork.*"

Being Bland CREATES: "Vanilla Nice" radio ads (quality, service and selection with our fast, friendly & knowledgeable staff!), boring, birdcage-bound brochures, weary web copy, limp logos and humdrum visuals that morph into the same "white noise" echoing throughout your market.

Being Bland MEANS: You will be ignored.

(Even if you slash your unbeatable, everyday low prices!)

Being Bland IS DEFINITELY: Bad for your business.

Being Bland KILLS: Any hope of your brand emerging as a recession-proof, ever growing and evolving community of loyal customers who generate long-term growth and profitability.

Being Bland IS: Going through the motions. Drowning in the "Sound of Silence".

Being Bland IS: Never once being able to "Shout it Out Loud" or lose your mind in "Detroit Rock City".

Being Bland IS: A public admission that you lack the vision, imagination and courage to come up with a fist-pumping, pelvic-humping brand message that rocks somebody's night-time world - including your own.

According to Dictionary.com, "bland" is defined a number of ways, including: Mild; tasteless; lacking in special interest, liveliness, individuality; insipid; dull; unemotional, indifferent, or casual.

If you want to get your business (and your brand) noticed by customers, future employees and inspire people already in your show, consider an approach to:

BE OUTRAGEOUS: Because it's the only place in your category that isn't already overcrowded.

BE OUTRAGEOUS: Because it beats the hell out of being boring.

BE OUTRAGEOUS: Because boring is risky as a brand strategy.

Unless, of course you want to blend in with the other "sphincterizing suits" and develop a non-offensive, guaranteed-never-to-shock brand, that settles for a peaceful, ordinary and most uneventful existence in the "Land of Bland". Consequences include getting blindsided someday by a competitor with the vision and gonads to be OUTRAGEOUS!

Being Bland IS: A choice.

Yours to make.

In the early 1970's, four guys named Peter, Paul, Ace and Gene made the outrageous choice to don colourful costumes, full make-up, 7-inch leather heels and strut through the streets of New York - BEFORE they cut their first record! The musical and theatrical juggernaut that emerged became known as "The hottest band in the land!" KISS owes its very existence to a willingness to accept the slings and the arrows that go with acting outrageously.

That's what got them noticed. That - and the fact that KISS could deliver unforgettable, larger-than-life performances - sealed their future as a band and as a brand. Even though the technology has changed from the days of albums and hit singles on the radio, the formula for outrageous success still holds true today.

No matter the industry or category.

For example, few pursuits are as full of intellectual and cultural snobs as the wine industry. It's a haven for tight-ass aficionados who get off displaying their intimate knowledge about the finer things in life, giving them the cheap thrill of looking down their long snooty noses at cultural riff raff who wouldn't know the difference between a Chablis and a Chardonnay.

The perfect arena for a controversial connoisseur to rock the boat.

Gary Vaynerchuk, host of WineLibraryTV (winelibrarytv.com) is a 32-year-old, in-your-face, New Yorker. He lives and dies with the on-field fortunes of the NFL Jets, often making mention of that fact in the more than 450 daily wine-tasting television shows he has appeared in online.

Gary Vee has borrowed at least a partial page from the KISS "shock 'em and rock 'em" philosophy, and become THE guy who uses the platform shoes of social media to become a bona-fide "Internet Rock Star".

His show, with an audience of 80,000 a day, has vaulted Vaynerchuk into the international spotlight. He has appeared on two of the biggest TV talk shows in the US and been featured in the Wall Street Journal and Time. Gary Vee has discovered there's more to using online video to sell wine - although it has helped a small family-owned store become a $60m-a-year enterprise. Calling himself "the social media sommelier", he says *"I'd rather have a million friends right now than a million dollars. Your social equity is far greater than your financial equity."*

The Web is fertile ground for those who can seamlessly transcend its reach from computer screens into the homes, minds, and hearts of the masses. Not only is he "Internet Famous," Gary's activities have flipped the pompous, stuffy wine industry on its head, opening the door to bring wine to the hearts, and palates, of everyday people. In other words, he has taken a web-based bazooka and blown centuries of real and perceived arrogance, snobbery and elitism out of the f%*&ing water. Like, Gene, Peter, Paul and Ace, those who don't like what he does can kiss his glass.

Gary not only broadcasts riveting, outrageous wine reviews daily, he adheres to the must-have elements for effective use of Social Media. Killer content and street cred earned through:

Transparency.
Authenticity.
Respect.
Trust.
Conversations.
Relationships.

Before thinking you can escape the "Land of Bland" by drinking social media "Kool-Aid", Vaynerchuk has proven you need to have something to say.

Something believable.

Something of value to any community you hope to gain any traction with. Maybe something OUTRAGEOUS!

But, Vaynerchuk isn't into Kool-Aid. Gary Vee is very much into wine.

He also swirls, swishes and spits it back out, sharing his very real reaction. He's not preaching or marketing at you. He's not selling you anything. He's sharing himself with you, providing content, value, and informed opinion. And he also listens to you through an on-line dialogue.

Some of his opinions about branding in the social media world may bother you. But it's highly doubtful that he gives a rat's ass.

"If you are a 32-year old guy that sleeps in the basement of your mom's house, in order to boycott reality TV, you are a few videos away from being the king of those people and becoming a cult star! Embrace who YOU are and WORK hard at it!"

YOU ARE THE BRAND!!! You don't need endorsements from people in your industry. Differentiate yourself! Don't buy lists, make lists!

The problem is, these companies don't want to work. They'd much rather give an agency $100,000 to run ads in the New York Post, commercials, pizza boxes, direct mail, and Stern radio ads, and they're done, right? They're clowns, don't feel bad for them. Let them die!" **-GARY VAYNERCHUK**

Have you noticed how much respect and utter admiration many of us have for the friend, foe, celebrity or colleague with the innate ability to "tell it like it is" and be completely candid? A visitor to www.seamlessbrand.blogpost.com commenting on this subject observed: *Wouldn't life be interesting if our filters were off more and blatant honesty was so revered and accepted that we all developed tougher skins? I would beg to assume that it would increase our productivity in so many ways. I am always amused when I am looking to be critiqued* constructively and I feel the truth eludes me even though I am begging for it....

Perhaps those sentiments explain why many appreciate what the Demon of Rock and Marketing Mastermind Gene Simmons posted in February 2009 on the subjects of life, business and branding:

"No one taught me what I know. I had to go out there, dig and scratch and scrounge up the bits and pieces of "the puzzle". And, it's never easy. Whenever I see new talent, or an ambitious young person, I always try to take time to sit, listen and then comment, critique, advise, offer some access when applicable. Because to become an entrepreneur, you must create your own business model, do your own research, fund it yourself and ultimately do it yourself.

And, this is not something you can learn in school. What I do isn't taught. I had to create myself. From top to bottom.

I gave myself the name Gene Simmons. I decided I didn't have to keep my given name. It didn't work. Yes. A name can help or hinder. It's your brand. And brands need to have something people respond to. Archibald Leech isn't as good as Cary Grant. Bernard Schwartz isn't as good as Tony Curtis. And Chaim Witz isn't as good as Gene Simmons.

I wanted to be in a rock band. But I also knew the world was filled with failed rock bands. So, the first thing was, to find band mates that shared a vision. Not an easy task. Then, find your position in the marketplace (who are you...what kind of band, who is your potential audience). It's almost impossible. But it IS possible. And only you have to decide all of the above and especially if you have the guts to devote the time, effort and the blood, sweat and tears (lots of em, don't worry) it takes to make it.

Thirty-five years later and KISS is about to embark on a Stadium Tour of South America, then swing up to Canada for some shows, then the US, Europe, Asia....But it's not the only thing I've done .I have managed other acts including LIZA MINNELLI, JENNI MULDAUR, DEAD OR ALIVE for a short time, and too many others to mention here. I discovered VAN HALEN. I started acting in movies and on TV. SIMMONS RECORDS has been reborn at Universal Music Canada. SIMMONS COMICS GROUP publishes three comic books, SIMMONS BOOKS recently published my 3rd Best Seller and with SIMMONS ABRAMSON MARKETING, we market and brand the IndyCar Series, including the Indy 500. We also represent FIND.COM. GENE SIMMONS FAMILY JEWELS (seen in 34 countries around the world).I created other TV Shows including MY DAD THE ROCK STAR, and then there is my clothing line with Canada's Dussault Custom Inc. as well as many keynote speaking engagements.

The above may come off as self serving. And, you're damn right it is. Some of you might think, "Who the hell does he think he is?" Precisely the point. Who DO you think you are? Are you special? Do you have the goods to stand in front of strangers and convince them you're what they need in their lives? That's always been my mantra. You buy the Vacuum Cleaner SALESMAN. Not the Vacuum Cleaner. It's the Messenger. NOT necessarily the message.

And the most important point -- the world doesn't need what you have to offer. You're not a farmer, policeman or teacher. They're important. You and I are not. What we do, the world could very easily live without. And yet, if you succeed, you can make more money, have more power and get better seats in restaurants than heads of state. IF you've got the goods and you're willing to work at it 24/7.....'til you drop dead .Vacation is for wimps. I've said my piece.

Your turn."

Gene Simmons has never experienced a shortage of self-confidence or a lack of critics. There would be as many people digesting this rant who admire Simmons and what he stands for as those who despise him. There aren't many who are indifferent when it comes to their opinion of the God of Thunder – either as a person or a brand. And that's part of the secret ingredient mixed into every great brand-building recipe.

TO BE OUTRAGEOUS: There is no in-between. It's black or white.

TO BE OUTRAGEOUS: Avoid the great divide; a swampy, Valley of Indifference lying between diametrically opposed emotional mountains called Love and Hate.

TO BE OUTRAGEOUS: Rock to the sound of your own music. March to the beat of your own Pearl drums.

The perceived safety of the "mushy middle", the "zone of mediocrity" has landed some of the world's biggest and most recognized brands on the scrap heap. K-Mart, John McCain, the Big Three Automakers and many others have learned the hard way how the Valley of Indifference becomes quicksand for a brand. Gene Simmons figured this shit out a long time ago. So has Gary Vee.

The degree to which someone pushes the brand envelope is usually in direct proportion to the level in which they feel secure in their own skin. Deep insecurities often manifest themselves in many businesses occupying "The Land of Bland" where anything bordering on OUTRAGEOUS is viewed with a mixture of hostility, disdain and envy.

KISS became the biggest-selling concert and merchandising act in the world, with over 2500 licensed products. Gary Vaynerchuk has taken the identical A.B.B. (Anything But Bland) approach in shocking sensibilities while attracting rabid viewers and escalating sales volumes.

How safe is "The Land of Bland"?

Only you know the answer.

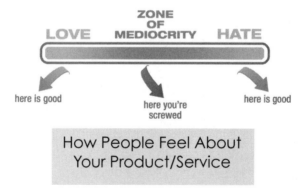

"James Bond has a license to kill, rock stars have a license to be outrageous. Rock is about grabbing people's attention."

-GENE SIMMONS

29
Ploughing the Road

"What you're talking about is like ploughing the road"

"What do you mean"?

"Well, it's kind of like when I was growing up in western Prince Edward Island and those days when we'd get hammered with about 4o inches of snow and my father would say, "somebody's gotta get out and start ploughing the road". The first pass was never perfect, edges were crooked and the plough may have knocked over the odd mailbox here and there, but they had to make the first run at it. Hours later another snow plough would come along and make the road a little wider and the edges a little straighter and before long people could drive again in relative comfort. But nothing happened till someone started ploughing the road"

With that story, Harvey captured a concept I had been sharing for years on the professional speaking and training circuit when it comes to attempting anything new that might take someone out of their comfort zone.

"Anything worth doing ... is worth doing badly".

Do something badly?

Absolutely.

In other words, can you jump in and do something badly (at first) as opposed to being paralyzed by a chronic need to have all your ducks in a row before starting a new project or learning a new skill? Just ask yourself how well did you play golf, swing a tennis racket, act in the school play; ski, skate or sketch the very first time? Can anyone expect to do anything well unless that "thing" is first performed "badly"?

Do something "badly" long enough, make enough mistakes, learn from them and you just might surprise yourself and others.

Willingness to attempt something new is what led Harvey to build his first "live-bottom" trailer in 1999 for a local lime hauler near Trout River, PEI. A conventional dump truck wasn't doing the job. Materials would clump and stick and there was a constant threat of the trailer tipping over. After looking the project over, Harvey took it upon himself to look at various "live-bottom" trailer concepts and by combining the best features from several designs, came up with the initial "Trout River Design".

Three years later, Harvey opened a manufacturing plant in tiny Coleman, PEI with floor space to build three trailers simultaneously. His design, which allows for a "seamless" and safe transfer of cargo, has caught on with carriers right across Canada, interested in protecting their profits and their drivers. By 2006, more than 40 people were employed at the expanded 30,000 square foot facility with more than 90% of their products sold out-of-province. Trout River Industries also has licensing agreements with companies as far away as Australia to build and sell their products worldwide, as web traffic steadily increases at www.troutriverindustries.ca.

In October of 2008, Harvey Stewart of Trout River Industries was recognized as the Ernst & Young Atlantic Manufacturing Entrepreneur of the Year at a black-tie gala in Halifax, Nova Scotia. "Ploughing the Road" has paid off handsomely for Harvey and his Western PEI team, in much the same way Chuck benefited from doing something "badly" more than 50 years ago, when he was starting to scratch out a living as an artist in California.

Chuck grew up in Spokane, Washington and moved with his parents to Los Angeles in the 1920's where his father made several, unsuccessful attempts trying to start his own business. Chuck's father would launch every new venture with new stationery and new pencils brandishing the company name. When the business failed, his father would quietly turn the huge stacks of useless stationery and pencils over to Chuck and his siblings, requiring them to use up all the material as fast as possible. Later, in one art school class, the professor gravely informed Chuck and his fellow students that they each had 100,000 bad drawings in them that they must first get past before they could possibly draw anything worthwhile. That one line spurred Chuck on, sometimes drawing and re-drawing his work again and again just so he could get that one perfect drawing. After graduating, Chuck Jones held a number of low-ranking jobs in the animation industry, eventually hitting his stride with a company named after a couple of brothers called Warner. He ploughed his way to success with a future, Oscar-winning rabbit named Bugs, a duck dubbed Daffy and other characters such as the Roadrunner and Wile E. Coyote.

Among his many works, *One Froggy Evening Duck Amuck* and *What's Opera Doc?* have been inducted into the National Film Registry. Asked once about his versions of Bugs Bunny and Daffy Duck, Jones has said, *"Bugs is who we want to be. Daffy is who we are."*

Whenever attempting something new, artists like Harvey and Chuck can assure you that it's only natural to expect to stumble. Or even fall flat on your face. There is vast evidence that even the most accomplished people need about ten years of hard work before becoming world-class. The pattern is so well established that researchers call it "the ten-year rule". As John Horn of the University of Southern California and Hiromi Masunaga of California State University observes, "The ten-year rule represents a very rough estimate, and most researchers regard it as a minimum, not an average". In "Outliers", Malcolm Gladwell contends 10,000 hours of rehearsal is the difference between success and non-success, genius and mediocrity. The New Yorker author maintains anyone from the Beatles to Bill Gates succeeded on the back of at least 10,000 hours of practice, as well as courage, passion and talent.

Tackling something difficult is a sign you're learning something new, because if it's too easy, it probably contains elements of what you already know. There is no way you can skid if you stay in a rut. The challenge lies in being able to distinguish the difference between a single detour and permanent defeat.

In which ways does your business and brand need to be "ploughing the road"? How willing are you to jump in and do something "badly" seeing it as but a small toll to pay to travel on the highway of excellence?

Ready to scribble 100,000 lousy drawings? Invest 10,000 lonely hours of preparation? Which new roads do you intend to "plough"? And should your "ploughing" ever stop?

Take action. Do something badly. Make mistakes. Gain experience.

The only person who avoids failure is the guy who fails to leave his driveway.

"You always pass failure on your way to success"
-MICKEY ROONEY

30
Load Warriors

"My rig's a little old but that don't mean she's slow. There's a flame from her stack and the smoke's rolling black as coal. My hometown's coming in sight, if you think I'm happy you're right. Six days on the road and I'm gonna make it home tonight." **-DAVE DUDLEY**

As you sip coffee from your cup each morning, have you ever stopped to contemplate the process involved in getting that mug in front of you?

In other words, the process and the people responsible for making sure your cup was able to leave some factory and wind up on a shelf at a store somewhere, where cash could be exchanged for that item.

This thrill ride usually begins with a phone call to a guy like Norm.

Norm works in the sales department. On the other end of the line is a mug manufacturer, needing to ensure sure those cups wind up on store shelves near you. And have them arrive on time and on budget. Depending on how Norm handles that conversation, the person on the other end of the line will move from being a prospect to becoming a paying customer, with a newly-created account ready to move your mug through the next fifteen steps of this process.

Julie will calculate the rates.
Ruth will input the billing.
Heather will ensure the bill gets paid.
Rod will involve customer service people.
Larry will allocate operational resources.
Mike will assign the drivers.
Gary will determine what's needed at the terminal.

Marie will enter and code the shipment.

Wayne will dispatch the load.

Brad will decide how the account is handled on the dock.

Joey will check off rigs entering and exiting the gate.

Dean will make sure forklift drivers are ready.

Brian will cross reference the waybill numbers.

Andrew will inspect the load to ensure proper packing.

And George will review the manifest; complete a pre-trip inspection of his tractor as well as the trailer, before confirming the trip with dispatch and hauling your mug and other freight through hundreds of miles of constantly changing weather and traffic conditions.

The above scenario is a mere snapshot of what unfolds behind-the-curtain, managing just one of more than 6,000 accounts served each day by Armour Transportation Systems. Headquartered in Moncton, NB, there are at least 16 major links in the Armour customer fulfillment chain, supporting more than 7,000 daily shipments, involving the work of 1700 employees at 23 terminals, achieving on-time performance ratings of more than 95%. All told these 16 links seamlessly work together to ship more than 9 billion pounds of freight annually.

Most business models have no more than 4 or 5 major links involved in completing a customer transaction. What makes Armour and many other companies in the trucking industry stand out is the understated and effective manner in which they get the job done.

Quietly winning far more battles than they lose each day.

Without any fanfare or hype.

"I'm a road hammer, a white knuckled steel gear jammer, Rig jockey highway slammer, I'm just doin' what I gotta do, I'm a road hammer, double talkin' CB grammar, Haul your load from Alabama all the way to Timbuktoo"

-THE ROAD HAMMERS

The Armour team is typical of the low-key Load Warriors of the North American economy; road hammers forging their craft on crowded freeways, silently toiling under the cultural, social and business radar.

Completing that staggering volume of customer transactions in such a seamless manner would see most companies placed on a corporate pedestal in much the same fashion as Apple, Oracle or Virgin. But when was the last time you saw a guy like Wes Armour or any other trucking tycoon splashed on the cover of major business magazines, idolized the same way as a Steve Jobs, Larry Ellison or Richard Branson? Chances are that won't happen anytime soon, because people in the transportation sector rarely beat their chests about how great they are and how the rest of the world needs to know it. As a group, folks with diesel in their DNA don't have time or inclination to boast. It's just not in their blue collar genes.

People in trucking - on and off the road – tend to let their work speak for itself.

Ask a group of 100 professional truckers - with more than a million accident-free miles under their belt - how many of them consider themselves to be "above average" drivers. You might see one or two raise their hands. Even though they have safely guided 70-ton payloads across thousands of miles, in all weather conditions, hardly any of them would consider themselves to be "special" in any way.

"It's all the same, only the names will change. Everyday it seems we're wasting away. Another place where the faces are so cold. I'd drive all night just to get back home. I'm a cowboy, on a steel horse I ride, I'm wanted dead or alive."

-JON BON JOVI

Some will quickly and casually dismiss trucking industry types as "rough around the edges" individuals who wound up where they are more by accident than by design. The way the media often portrays it, truckers are unskilled, big bellied brutes who hog the road, take up too much room and drive too fast. "Fat Finger Freddie's" who only listen to two kinds of music: Country and Western.

This, from a recent conversation, overheard at Starbucks:

*"Well, ya know Joey could always get a get a job drivin'
a truck. It's not like you need to be educated or nothin' and
he'd fit right in. It's not like what you would call a professional
environment where ya need a degree. Just gotta know how to
drive and move shit around."*

However, many "educated" business professionals would be
hard-pressed to put down their lattes long enough to duplicate
the track record of efficiency established at Armour and many
other companies in the transportation industry. The white collar
world would also struggle to match the unique mix of systemic
sophistication and salt-of-the-earth humility you will find in the
trucking business. What you will discover is otherwise ordinary,
everyday people doing extraordinary work.

Take a moment and look around at the items surrounding
you right now in your home or office. Whether it's that cup you
are holding, that chair you are sitting on or that computer you
are staring at, it's fair to say...

"If you bought it, a truck brought it."

Our entire economy depends on a network of logistical,
mechanical and human systems far more complex than a
bunch of redneck, beer-bellied rig jockeys jamming gears,
riding steel horses from Point-A to Point-B. It must be tough some
days to keep a cool head and be patient with civilian drivers
who curse or flip the bird to the big rig drivers who play such a
significant role in putting groceries on their table or delivering
the myriad of gifts they bought for their kid's birthday.

Millions are blinded to the bigger economic picture any
driver sees from up in the cab every day. Trucking people
frequently have a better grasp than Wall Street bankers on
where the economy is heading - simply by paying attention to
what gets loaded on their trailers each and every day.

Next time you jump into the hammer lane to pass an
18-wheeler with a 53-foot billboard, think about the team behind
that long hauler making it all possible. Consider the many hidden
links in the chain supporting that load and the often thankless,
far from glamorous jobs people do, making sure the wheels of
commerce keep turning for all of us.

How does your customer fulfillment track record match up with what trucking professionals accomplish as a matter of routine each day?

Is there something your business could learn from these heroes of the highway?

PRAYER OF A TRUCK DRIVER'S WIFE

"Please bless my husband while he's out on the road. Please protect him from the wind and rain and cold. Help him to keep that big rig between the white lines so he can make it to his destination on time. May he find his back-haul quickly and make it home soon. Please light his night on the road with your stars and moon. Let him rest peacefully in his sleeper's bed, and please let there be a good meal and fresh coffee at the truck stop ahead. Help me to keep the home fires burning while he's out there movin' on. And give me the strength and wisdom to take care of things while he's gone. May the road he travels be clear and dry, and may not temptation catch his eye. Help him remember when he's all alone that his loving wife and best friend is waiting for him here at home"

-LINDA SMITH

31
Branding in a Recession

Do you know the difference between a recession and a depression?

Perhaps the easiest way to distinguish the two is to think about it this way:

In a recession, your neighbour loses his job; in a depression, you lose yours!

The National Bureau of Economic Research (NBER) confirmed on December 1, 2008, that the U.S. economy has been in a recession since December 2007. Many economists believe this recession to be the worst since the recession of 1981-82.

But tough times don't last. Tough people do.

And the lessons of history become even more valuable when you contemplate how life changes in a business ocean suddenly pounded by economic storm conditions. In every recession, the ocean (your market) that has sustained you and your competitors shrinks to the size of a pond - and that spells trouble for those who can't foresee the implications of this contraction. Natural law dictates that some companies (smaller, slower fish) will be squeezed out of the pond, gasping, choking and wheezing before washing ashore on the beaches of bankruptcy.

A natural, knee-jerk reaction to this "shrinking pond" dynamic would be to cut back on branding activities, such as marketing, advertising, P.R., and a new darling, social media. However, the patterns of history and countless studies have shown taking your foot off the branding gas pedal might be the most dangerous thing you can do for your enterprise in tough economic times.

In a study of U.S. recessions, McGraw-Hill Research analyzed 600 companies from 1980-1985. The results showed that companies that maintained or increased advertising budgets during the 1981-82 recession averaged *significantly higher sales growth,* both during the recession and for the following three years, than those that eliminated or decreased advertising. By 1985, sales of companies that were 'aggressive recession advertisers' had climbed 256% over those that didn't keep up their advertising.

But wait ... there's more!

Another series of six studies conducted by the research firm of Meldrum & Fewsmith showed conclusively that advertising aggressively during a recession not only boosted sales, but also increased profits and overall market share. This fact has held true for all post-World War II recessions studied by The American Business Press starting in 1949.

In fact, looking back as far as the Great Depression, there is a core group of companies that appear to rub their marketing mitts with glee every time the economic storm clouds gather. The list includes Campbell Soup, Coca-Cola, Gillette, Nabisco and others, but perhaps no one has consistently demonstrated the effectiveness of boosting branding activities when a boom goes bust than Procter and Gamble. Back in the "dirty thirties" P&G president Richard Deupree believed people were still buying essential household products and saw the opportunity to capture market share, despite protests to cut back on advertising from shareholders. Instead, P & G floored it, investing in a new medium called "radio" and sponsored programs built around a new format that concentrated heavily on personal and family "drama". The first P&G sponsored program, "Ma Perkins" debuted thanks to the good folks from Oxydol. Sensing they had a hit on their hands, P&G went on to develop shows for Ivory Soap, Camay and other brands, virtually doubling radio spending every two years during the depression. By the time World War II opened in 1939, Procter & Gamble was sponsoring no fewer than 21 radio programs while helping to create what would become forever known as "soap operas".

When the pond is shrinking, there are fewer competitors with the gills to splash around and make some noise. Consequently, your message has a better chance of being heard and when the tidal wave of prosperity comes rushing back in (which it always has in the 35 recessions since 1867), your brand has a window of opportunity to leapfrog over everybody else; to

180

become the ONE brand customers in your category think of first.

- Everyone still needs to put gas in the car.
- Families still need to buy groceries.
- Kids still need clothes and school supplies.
- Handymen still need power tools and other gadgets.
- Women still need makeup and lipstick.
- NFL fans still need new Jalapeno-flavoured Doritos chips.
- And great brands still need to flourish and grow.

Here is why:

When times are good, your branding activities - marketing, advertising, social media and public relations strategies - set you apart from the other fish. When times are tough, those same branding activities allow you to gain an unbeatable advantage once the inevitable rush of fresh water from the turnaround arrives.

It is vital to remember that during a recession the consumer doesn't go away. Instead he becomes more discerning. He starts working harder to find the "V' word – Value. He will hold on to his stuff a little longer, repair rather than replace, shop around and compare prices and find a way to justify "affordable luxuries" like booze and a night at the movies.

Is your business model, its products and services able to withstand that type of scrutiny? Are you nimble enough to be able to respond quickly in the face of increased opportunities and threats anytime economic uncertainty turns turbulent? Have you built up enough brand equity to sustain your business through periodic rough spots beyond your current control?

Whenever economic doom and gloom dominates headlines, it's a sure indication that market share is up for sale.

The only question is which brands will flee to the shallow end and which will bravely face the waves and swim out to deeper water?

"I have learned, that if one advances confidently in the direction of his dreams, and endeavors to live the life he has imagined, he will meet with a success unexpected in common hours." **-HENRY DAVID THOREAU**

32
Christmas Eve, 1971

It was a Christmas Eve theweatherman had decided to frown upon.

Sleet and freezing rain pelted the city of just over 100,000 souls, a blue-collar type of town that included two lonely gas jockeys working the graveyard shift.

Somewhere around 11 o'clock that evening, a well-heeled chap, firmly into his seventies, pulled up to the service station.

He was driving a shiny blue Meteor.

Elegantly attired wife by his side.

The dapper elderly gent bounced into the glassed-in cubicle perched on the gas island - more of an over sized phone booth - and after wishing the occupants a Merry Christmas, asked "How's business?" Almost simultaneously, the phone rang and the caller asked the gas attendant if he could send a tow truck to the nearby St. Rose Church. He and his family had just left the 10 o'clock Christmas mass and unfortunately, their vehicle was now stuck in an unforgiving snow bank.

"I'm sorry sir but we don't have a tow truck and besides, there is nobody else open. It's Christmas Eve after all. There really isn't much we can do"

The telephone was placed back on the receiver.

The elderly gentleman, having overheard the conversation asked "What was that all about?" The 17-year old attendant stammered and explained the situation, adding he couldn't' help since there were no resources at his disposal. And hey, it was Christmas Eve.

The gentleman, whose name was Kenneth, looked around, spied some 20-pound bags of rock salt and without a pause, ordered the two attendants to load several bags into his trunk. He paid for the merchandise, confirmed directions to the church and in a flash he and the missus were off to render assistance to the stranded family.

Three decades later, hundreds of people in the company that bears his name are still talking about what happened on Christmas Eve 1971 in Saint John, New Brunswick.

One can only imagine the look on the stranded driver's face when no more than five minutes after calling an Irving service station a few blocks away, none other than an angel named Kenneth Colin showed up to help dig him and his family out. It was as though the Star of Bethlehem itself was shining on this deserted family, trapped in a snow bank, praying for a miracle.

Kenneth Colin.

Otherwise known as "KC"

As in Irving.

Upon hearing what had happened, the lesson of what had just transpired gradually began to dawn on the 17-year old named Joel.

"This guy will never be able to buy anything but Irving gas and Irving home heating fuel for the rest of his life. That's brilliant"

By the time the events of Christmas Eve 1971 had unfolded, KC Irving had already accomplished more than most would dream of accomplishing in a lifetime. To those who knew him, the humility of his deeds that evening was hardly surprising. KC's own beginnings were humble, running the family business in his tiny hometown of Bouctouche, New Brunswick in the early 1920's. A born tinkerer, Irving was fascinated by the automobile and eventually added a service station and a Ford dealership. In 1925 Irving's commitment to expansion was evident as he opened a second service station in Saint John.

KC would go on to forge a business empire rivalled by few, with an enduring legacy that has touched thousands of livelihoods and communities all over Atlantic Canada and beyond. Considered one of the foremost entrepreneurs of the 20th century, he became one of the world's leading industrialists with Forbes magazine pegging him as one of the wealthiest men in the world, with assets of $9 billion in U.S. dollars in 1988.

In 1989, he was made an Officer of the Order of Canada.

To a young, impressionable Joel Levesque, who would eventually become one of Canada's top public relations experts with Moosehead Breweries, the mental imprint of what took place on that otherwise bitterly cold and cruel Christmas Eve has never left.

Perhaps it is one of the greatest business lessons of all time from one of its greatest masters.

And it's a lesson KC captured one day in '24 when he put pen to paper: *"Look after the customer ... and they'll look after you"*

Legend has it that when KC was a boy, the noise of the pet ducks which he was raising in the family garden brought complaints from neighbours. Demonstrating his business sense at an early age, the young Irving promptly had the fowl butchered, sold them to the neighbours, solving the problem and netting himself a $100 profit for his efforts. In later years, many of his critics called KC a cranky old bastard who cared only about cash - the Atlantic Canada's answer to Scrooge McDuck and the Grinch all rolled up into one.

Last time I checked, no one erects a statue to honour a critic.

Actions always speak louder than words.

Say what you will about Kenneth, but if nothing else, he was a doer of deeds who always cared about his customer. Including the one who may not have bought a thing that snowy day - but who just might be back tomorrow.

How far will your business go to "look after the customer"?

What would that do for your brand?

Are there more lessons from this story than meets the eye?

"Numbers don't mean anything. Its people who count." **-WILL ROGERS**

33
A Taste of PGU

"You quickly realize you are part of something really big".

"Anybody coming in to PGU can see it doesn't matter what business experience you have, something is going to hit you right between the eyes".

"This is the most fun I've ever had with my clothes on"

Nancy didn't know what to make of the way things are done at PropertyGuys.com University. When the limo dropped her off on Day One, no more than 20 minutes had elapsed before she realized this was a very different type of training class. This would not be just another manic Monday as she began to experience a curriculum that includes:

- Mock drafts to choose teams.
- Hands-on, experiential exercises with monikers like "Breaking the Ice", "Thursday Morning Quarterback" and "Shane's House of Pain".
- Competition-based case studies
- Video-taped media interviews.
- Class nicknames, awards, songs and logos.
- A choice between red or white wine.

For most of her adult life, Nancy could be described as quiet, reserved, somewhat shy, and now here she was faced with the challenge of competing in an "American Idol" type competition, designed to transfer emotional knowledge about the inner workings of Canada's real estate industry. Her initial foray into "The House of Pain" was anything but a walk in the park.

In fact, Nancy could not, would not go through with it.

Frozen solid by shivering waves of fear, angst and worry.

Nothing in her academic upbringing had prepared her for anything like this.

However, over the course of a week at PGU, Nancy, learned how to stretch her personal comfort zone to the point where on Thursday night, she was walking with a much different step. What was ordinarily an anxiety-filled exercise in self-consciousness had disappeared entirely. (Yes, there are people so troubled by what on-lookers might be thinking, they find it difficult just to enter a pub). Nancy breezed in with a confident stride, effortlessly making her way through the crowded establishment as she joined new friends for dinner and drinks.

"You go girl!

Traditional business training programs are little more than product knowledge information dumps complete with checklists, rules and procedures. PropertyGuys.com University takes a different approach, leveraging timeless principles that promote critical thinking and the value of intuition. Mounting research suggests, developing emotional intelligence, even more so than IQ, contributes greatly to helping someone like Nancy become an outstanding performer at work. In his book, *Emotional Intelligence*, author Daniel Goleman argues social intelligence and emotional competencies are not innate talents, but rather learned capabilities that can be developed to achieve outstanding career and life performance.

PropertyGuys.com University, headquartered in Moncton, N.B., is one example of a trend towards creating Conceptual Age Colleges that place a priority on developing much more than a person's ability to know the technical aspects of any job. "How's and "what's" are relegated to secondary status. Instead, PGU faculty delivers a program that keys on "why" things are done a certain way, designed to accelerate adult learning in critical areas such as self-confidence, curiosity, presentation skills, collaborating with others and being able to intuitively recognize patterns of business opportunity.

How would enhancing those qualities benefit your brand?

What if you took a moment right now to experience a Conceptual Age approach to learning?

Hey, there is no better time than the present.

According to the latest research, what portion of career success can be attributed to I.Q.? (Intelligence Quotient)

a) 50 to 60 percent
b) 35 to 45 percent
c) 23 to 29 percent
d) 15 to 20 percent

Before we share the answer, stop for a moment and consider the way you process the question in the first place. In all probability, the way you responded likely reflects a path followed through 20th century educational systems that got you to where you are today. Like most, you spent thousands of hours in classrooms, listening to lectures, digesting dusty, chunky textbooks, routinely completing batteries of tests and exams. Typically, these exercises in learning offered multiple choice or fill-in-the-blank questions in an effort to confirm to the people in charge how much knowledge you had acquired.

But did any real learning take place?

Or did you just hone your ability to memorize and regurgitate?

In his best-seller, "A Whole New Mind", Daniel Pink argues the Industrial and Information Ages that characterized the previous millennium has given way to what he calls the Conceptual Age. In the Industrial Age, assembly line workers using physical strength emerged as main players only to be replaced by knowledge workers of the Information Age; accountants, lawyers, doctors, engineers, professors or business executives. By and large these were the shiny products of logic- based, factory models of education, geared towards "left-brain" attributes such as analytical thinking and deductive reasoning. Ideal for producing students who know *what* to do without necessarily understanding the all-encompassing question of *why*.

"There's a battle outside, and it is ragin'. It'll soon shake your windows and rattle your walls, for the times they are a-changin"
-BOB DYLAN

You don't need a rock legend crooning in your ear to know, the economic times and business landscape has been a changin'.

Daniel has seen how the lines have been drawn and the curse has been cast.

A former speechwriter for Al Gore, Pink maintains the ability to see the "bigger picture" is increasingly vital as a response to global competition and the demands of a hurtling, turbulent digital economy. He sees a shift already upon us where the Information Age, and its emphasis on logical, linear, rational thinking, transitions to the "Conceptual Age," where "right-brain" qualities like empathy, inventiveness and intuition take centre stage. He contends the future belongs to a different type of person applying creative skills such as design, story-telling and a capacity to intuitively detect patterns and opportunities.

Companies like PropertyGuys.com, determined to stay ahead of that curve, are responding by creating their own Conceptual Age Colleges. Imagine a week-long program where students travel to-and-from class via stretch limousine and introduced to a dynamic, interactive curriculum that leaves many shaking their heads in wonder. A school where "a-ha moments" happen with enough regularity that graduates like Nancy refer to the unconventional, unpredictable and unforgettable week at PGU as life-changing. Graduates depart as accredited Private Sale Professionals, ready to apply a new level of conceptual thinking critical to business success.

The founders of PropertyGuys.com based their model on a school founded in 1961 by another small, growing company that was determined to become a franchising behemoth. While some initially snickered about obtaining a degree in Hamburgerology, McDonald's first corporate school in a Chicago suburb offered a detailed, two-week curriculum for a class of 15 students.

Today, Hamburger University sits on an 80-acre campus, with a state-of-the-art facility that includes 13 teaching rooms, a 300 seat auditorium, 12 interactive education team rooms, and 3 kitchen labs. Translators can provide simultaneous translation, and the faculty of 30 resident professors has the ability to teach in 28 different languages.

In all likelihood, McDonald's visionary Ray Kroc performed a little R &D (Rob and Duplicate) in borrowing the idea from America's first corporate university. Walt realized the need for a structured learning environment to teach the unique skills

188

required of Disney cast members. And to this day, all new employees, otherwise known as cast members, go through identical one-and-a-half day training program called *Traditions* where they learn the basics of how the Disney brand meets and exceeds guest expectations at the front-line.

Walt, Ray and Ken know building great brands works best when you build from the inside-out.

Companies like PropertyGuys.com are remarkable in the way they adapt proven formulas from icons such as McDonald's and Disney in a way that fits their own unique culture and the realities of the 21st century. CEO Ken LeBlanc credits PGU as a key to PropertyGuys.com become the first company from Atlantic Canada to win the 2008 Canadian Franchise Association Award of Excellence. LeBlanc believes weaving brand spirit into the fabric of franchisees from the beginning is what sets the stage to develop a business that has broken records for franchise sales, garnered national awards and media attention while steadily growing market share in the ultra-competitive real estate industry.

Before we forget, here is the answer to the earlier, multiple-choice question:

Between 4 and 10 percent.

According to Daniel Goleman, confining oneself solely to the choices being offered is a symptom of excessive, logical-based thinking as opposed to abstract, conceptual-based thinking. The ability to see other solutions and possibilities without being locked into fixed, mental positions.

Are you creating an internal brand based on possibilities or predictability?

That may hinge on whether you see orientation, training & development as a budget-busting frill or an unnecessary expense. Or perhaps, you're hoping and praying government-run education systems will somehow satiate the ravenous hunger that growing companies have for talented, creative people.

Be sure to let us know how that works out for you.

"We're failing our children, especially our young men. We provide them a cognitive, analytical education, but we fail to educate their emotions. If I had one wish, it would be that we immerse our children in a performance of the arts. Let a storyteller or a poet perform in a way that leaves the audience breathless and every child in the room will say, 'I want to learn to do that.' They'll become better readers, better writers, more complete human beings" **-DANA GIOIA**

Will your business be able to compete on a global stage in a Digital Economy with products of left-brain dominant education systems that stunt right-brain creativity? At what point does your brand take the business of education into its own hands? Education does cost money but what is the price of ignorance?

Do you look at the growth and development of people like Nancy as integral to building a brand that will stand the test of time? Can you envision the magic of Disney combined with the efficiencies of McDonalds happening within your own Conceptual Age College?

PropertyGuys.com could see the potential with PGU. It continues to be a key element in shaping its brand in a seamless fashion.

What possibilities can you picture for your brand?

"I would rather be green and growing than ripe and rotting" **-RAY KROC**

A Note From a PGU Graduate

April 24, 2009
Hey Ken,

I just wanted to thank you for the card and
the $50. The $50 was great but more important
was the recognition. My confidence, not only in our product,
but in myself grows each day. You have an incredible team,
and the message and training I am getting is top notch. My
previous employer is a Fortune 500 company and one of
Canada's top 50 employers. I went through over 400 hrs of
training in the 12 years that I was there and I could hardly
stay awake 10 minutes for any of it. Your program makes
them look like small cap, amateurs. My week here is flying
by and as Shane said I would, I am having a great time and
learning a lot. The learning is only part of it though. Being
here, experiencing the vibe, the team work and the positive
attitudes is contagious. My fellow classmates and I were
complete strangers coming in to this and after day 3, they are
not only my colleagues, they are my friends. I am sure that they
are feeling it too. You have developed an amazing corporate
culture that I am sure you are proud of. I feel sorry for those
that will have to do this program online in the future. More
importantly, I feel fortunate to be able to be here in Moncton
NB (yes, I am serious) experiencing it, live, and in person. I
came in to PGU still having some reservations and doubt; I will
be leaving as a strong believer, with limitless ambition.

Once again, thank you.
Sincerely,
Jeremy

191

BONUS SECTION

"I looked at Mick Jagger and Keith Richards and the boys up there thinking, I want to be that"

-SAMMY HAGAR

34
The Seamless Brand

January 27, 2009.

At the Mayan Riviera Resort in sunny Mexico.

A guest speaker is addressing a national franchise conference on the subject of Human Resources and internal branding. He shares a story about a customer who called WestJet one day to file a complaint. The speaker reads from a letter that had been subsequently mailed in by the unhappy customer.

"Back in November 2006, I called your head office to voice a complaint regarding my friends' flight. I was upset and ended up speaking to a supervisor by the name of Lisa Cooper. While she was pleasant to deal with, that is not the reason that I am writing this letter. I was quite frustrated when I called, but Lisa remained even and calm throughout our conversation. About halfway through our discussion, my 4-year old son picked up the phone, and began chattering away. Despite my attempts to shush him off, he was adamant that it was time for me to go, as it was Sunday, and the NASCAR race was coming on TV. Lisa chuckled at this, and explained, she too was a NASCAR fan. She asked my son who his favourite driver was, and it was quite the coincidence that it was hers as well, Jeff Gordon. My son immediately became excited and told her everything this 4-year old mind knew about the sport and the driver.

By this time, my initial concerns had been alleviated, but Lisa continued to take time out of her day to speak to my son, and make him feel special. I could see from across the room that he was wearing a grin from ear to ear. What Lisa didn't know at that time, was that I often didn't have the opportunity to see my son happy, as he was typically feeling the affects of leukemia. For 10 minutes, all of his pain and suffering was forgotten, as he slipped away into a story Lisa told about a NASCAR race in Las Vegas, and a friend of hers who drove "big boy cars", like Jeff Gordon.

For two weeks following that phone call, my son could do nothing but talk about the lady at WestJet who liked Jeff Gordon. Imagine his surprise on the day a small package arrived in the mail, from WestJet, addressed directly to him. He was ecstatic when he opened it to find a signed Jeff Gordon driver card, and a miniature Jeff Gordon car, along with an autographed photo of Lisa's friend who raced as well. Also included was a small Jeff Gordon teddy bear.

What made this extremely special was that our family lacked the extra finances to buy things such as these for our son, due to the high cost of medical bills.

For weeks on end, my son played with that car, stared at those photos and "Jeffie" the bear accompanied him to the hospital for each of his treatments. In early December, my boy and I sat on the floor in his bedroom, having just returned from the hospital, playing with his car. As I tucked him into bed that night, and kissed him on the forehead, he told me he loved his car, and as he curled up and went to sleep, he whispered, "Tell Lisa thank you Dad. I love you."

Tragically, my angel passed away that night.

In the weeks and months that followed, the only solace I found was in recalling the slight smile my baby had on his face, as he laid sleeping with the teddy bear tucked in next to him with the race car clutched in his hand.

For years now, I've only shared this story with close friends and family, as the pain of losing a child is often too hard to cope with. In the back of my mind though, I've always known that I would share this story with WestJet. I called in the other day, to ensure Lisa still worked there. Though the agent I spoke with did not know her personally, she assured me Lisa was still in head office. The agent also provided me the name of a manager, and I am hoping this letter will be directed to the right person.

I want Lisa to know that her small actions, helped to shape the last days of a young child, into something that will never be forgotten.

Sincerely,
Smith

Understandably, the speaker struggled to maintain composure through certain parts of this poignant story, but the overall message was not lost on his audience that morning. Choking back waves of emotion, it was abundantly clear that deeper connections were being made and understood throughout the conference room.

A "brand" has the potential to be much more than a logo, tagline or advertising strategy. A "brand" can represent much more than financial transactions involving products and services.

And a "seamless" brand like WestJet, with people like Lisa, demonstrate how branding can be elevated to an entirely different level.

Filed in a category marked "exceptional", Lisa's story is, nevertheless but one of thousands that unfold each month with the many special ways WestJetters interact with their customers one-on-one. The flight attendants who crack the corny jokes are just a slice of the overall corporate culture and strong brand identity of an organization that cares.

Employees are the heart and collective soul of any company, particularly in service businesses, where people ultimately deliver a brand promise. They shape the brand experience with each customer contact and for companies like WestJet; it is employees like Lisa who become its most memorable voice.

The front line of any firm has to believe in what a company stands for, live the brand promise and understand how they fit into its delivery. Only then, can brand supporting behavior start to gel, with a winning spirit that energizes every element of how a company. Only then, can a brand flourish in a "seamless" fashion that links internal culture to what marketing is communicating externally.

Which begs a question when it comes to you and your organization?

Who controls your brand?

Is it?

a) Your customers?

b) Your employees?

c) The media?

d) All of the above?

e) None of the above?

A multitude of forces affect how your brand is received and perceived, but you are still in control of your products and services. Still in control of the way they are packaged and distributed. And still in control of how you develop and communicate a brand promise and ensure those promises are kept.

But something has changed.

There was a time, way back when, (prior to 2000 B.G. – Before Google) a customer would complain only to see that concern disappear in a file folder or wastepaper basket somewhere. This was a time when employees were much more compliant and far less likely to rock any boats. But now, both your customers and employees have access to a stack of Marshall amplifiers - called "The Internet" - where everybody and anybody can riff about your brand.

You can't hide in a global, virtual world.

Not when your brand is what the roaring crowd at Google, LinkedIn, MySpace and Facebook says it is.

Are you ready to wake up and smell the flatness?

Or be the stubborn guardian of an impervious "I am a Rock" type of company, protected by hierarchical organizational fortresses deep and mighty?

Best-selling author Thomas Friedman contends in The World is Flat, that traditional hierarchies have been "flattened" forever, not just for countries and corporations, but for individuals.

"I am hoping, though, that many of them have kids, who, when they have a moment to take a break from their iPods, Internet, or Google, will explain to their parents running the country just how the world is being flattened."

-THOMAS FRIEDMAN

The impact of how the Internet affects business operations and how a brand develops is staggering. Forces of change now spread from the bottom-up and move side-to-side in a global, yet horizontal fashion – not top-down and vertical. The web itself is a seamless platform, creating seamless networks and communities. But, how can your brand become seamlessly connected with customers, employees, suppliers, potential talent and investors, like a WestJet for example, if it operates in a top-down, vertical, fashion?

197

And what if the "Flat World" concept flies in the face of how you view the basic structure and essence of an organization to begin with?

For most, our beliefs about the way organizations operate can be traced to automatic, visual interpretations of the way we think it's supposed to work. Usually, this mental image takes form in a top-down, vertically-driven organizational chart. There are functional areas like finance, marketing, operations, sales, human resources, etc, with each segment offering its own degree of expertise, specialized training, unique language and culture. Is it possible our perspective on this traditional, hierarchical structure is the underlying factor that creates cultures of "command and control" fostering real or imagined silos??

Think about organizations you have been a part of - or close enough to – to witness this dynamic. A lot of ass kissed on the way up. Plenty of shit shoveled on the way down. Words like "collaboration" and "alignment" may appear on pompous mission statements - but in reality, most people do just what the boss tells them to do. Yes sir, no sir, three bags full. Hardly an environment to harvest the potential of collective intelligence.

Could it be that a mental image of what people believe an organization to be, unwittingly prevent the whole from becoming greater than the sum of its parts?

What if you looked at organizational structures differently?

What if you envisioned an entirely new framework that allowed you to duplicate "seamless" models where diverse pieces of a business come together to form a consistent, authentic and transparent brand experience?

A key inspiration for The Seamless Brand™ as both a concept and business growth model can be discovered in the unique cultural and marketing approach employed by WestJet. As of 2008, the Calgary-based airline ranked as the 4th most profitable in the world. Over time, any one watching closely enough would notice how disparate elements such as the way you are treated at the call centre, to the check-in, from inside the cabin to what you see on the television commercials, are somehow, seamlessly interwoven at WestJet. It's as though one performance is being played out on many different stages by many different actors. All taking cues from the same script.

Everywhere you look or turn - over, under, upside down - from the WestJet "Big Shots" to the guys handling baggage or the "bean counters" in accounting, this brand has succeeded in inspiring Lisa and thousands of other WestJetters to operate from a uniform, emotional source code. But using some real R & D (robbing and duplicating) you too can develop a basic framework for recognizing how your brand can become "seamless".

Years of research, along with successful experimentation on the business frontlines, generated the development of this Seamless Brand™ framework. The business case for such a model is intriguing. Recent research from Harvard University indicates that anywhere from 70-to-80% of brand perception is determined by experiences with front-line people. Companies that create environments that produce vibrant, integrated cultures tend to outperform companies that don't by as much as five to six times.

It is virtually impossible to comprehend the pieces of any puzzle without seeing the entire picture. And that process begins with an unusual level of clarity that comes from being able to tap into a deeper, emotional source that is your brand and applying it in a consistent, seamless fashion in the key areas your promise has impact. Regardless of how technology and market conditions change, business models and brand promises will always originate with ideas born in someone's imagination. Those ideas need to resonate with real human beings who buy products and services and seek out career opportunities.

Here is what you already know: Making a promise is easy.

But, keeping a promise?

Different story altogether.

On a personal level, some of the promises we break to ourselves and each other on a daily basis probably won't cause the earth to spin off its axis.

But, if we're talking about building a remarkable brand - a promise not only has to be kept, it actually has to count for something. It needs to matter. This fundamental understanding is what allows organizations such as Disney, FedEx, Apple and WestJet to reach the stratosphere in building strong customer loyalty. That being said, communicating the brand promise and ensuring its consistent delivery, is the issue that causes business owners and their people more headaches than any other.

As mentioned earlier, part of the challenge lies in how organizational structures are perceived in our imagination. Top-down, vertical pyramids tend to automatically kick end-users to the bottom of any food chain. And if this structure is what drives behavior inside a company, brand breakage naturally occurs – despite slogans and posters, preaching "empowerment" or claiming "Our Customers Are #1". While top-down models worked like a charm during the Industrial Revolution, the "flat world" of the 21st century Digital Economy, demands a new perspective for brands that aspire to become "seamless".

Instead of "command and control" from the top, what if "brand essence", that flows from the centre, was the rallying point? Imagine looking at your organization this way:

A Seamless Brand™ operates on the principle that an intangible as "essence" - unifying particles of human energy and emotion - is what draws four distinct elements together. Conceptually, this compares favorably to what ancient Chinese referred to as the Tao, that nameless, colorless source with no shape or form which becomes the centre of everything you do in your business and everyone it impacts. Think of your brand as one that exists in timeless, boundless dimensions. Perfectly still, yet constantly moving. Hidden -yet always present.

Quantum physicists might refer to this nucleus as an energy source. Hopeless romantics will be tempted to wax poetic and speak the language of love. Philosophers may ponder possibilities of existential spirit. Call it what you will - brand persona, character or mojo - it is critical to recognize the existence of an intangible essence fuelling your brand promise. Companies unaware or in denial of this indescribable presence are likely the same ones that view its customers as a series of impersonal transactions - and its own people as a revolving door of disposable commodities. This ignorance or refusal is what wrings any shred of humanity out of a business, much like squeezing water from a sponge.

The framework of a Seamless Brand™ makes this intangible source code the focal point for attracting and holding the attention of four distinct elements.

These diverse, yet interrelated forces take shape this way:

- External Brand (current and future customers; potential employees)
- Internal Brand (senior executives; supervisors; front-line; the team)
- Individual Brand (employees; real people with their own aspirations)
- Executive Brand (owners; senior execs who inspire and share vision)

Identifying and plugging into your "source" is what allows your brand story to spread virally, get your business noticed, attract great talent and align your people. It becomes the spirit that energizes each and every function of your business as it strives to achieve the defining principle of a Seamless Brand™:

Make and Keep a Promise that Matters to your Customer.

That's it.

Make a promise that matters.

And then, keep it.

Brand strength always hinges on the level of trust and confidence it inspires in the marketplace. In his best-seller The

Speed of Trust, Stephen M.R. Covey argues, "Trust is a hard edged economic driver because it always addresses speed and cost." As Covey points out, when trust levels plummet, things that need getting done, take longer to happen, thus reducing speed while increasing costs. But the reverse is also true. In high trust environments, things get done faster, lowering cost. Consequently, in the new, flat world, Digital Economy, trust becomes the key currency in acquiring and keeping customers as well as inspiring and retaining talented team members.

It has been proven on countless occasions that faster, more passionate companies beat slower moving competitors plagued with low-morale. Once it is clearly understood that all brands – big and small – can generate speed and passion from this straightforward concept, attracting customers and engaging employees is somewhat simplified. Not necessarily easy, but at least the "seamless" model becomes a starting point to foster a remarkable story worthy of other people talking and writing about.

If a brand isn't lived on the inside, there is no way it can thrive on the outside.

In early 2005, for example, WestJet showed its employees a preview of three agency-created TV ads. But, they found the humor offensive and felt the ads did not align with their view of the brand. The result? The proposed ads were scrapped and although it meant starting from scratch, WestJet hit pay dirt with a new campaign that focused on employees as owners.

Unless a brand is built first from within, few will believe it. How many people do you know crave cheap gimmicks or generic sameness?

So what exactly makes your brand new, better or different compared to your direct and indirect competitors? Have you determined what your brand stands for? More importantly, what will it stand against?

In other words, what are the unshakeable, non negotiable standards that will define on a personal level how you do business?

No doubt, Lisa Cooper would have had other things happening in her life the day she decided to connect in a meaningful way with a 4-year who was not likely to be a paying customer any time soon. There was also no way on earth, Lisa could have known that the teddy bear she sent would be in the boy's arms the night he passed away. But, if you honestly see yourself as the owner of a company you care about, the essence of what your brand is all about will speak louder than any marketing or mission statement ever will.

Do you have a vision that will inspire people like Lisa to go out of their way to "be the brand"?

Is there a "values mountain" she and others will see you are prepared to plant a flag and die for?

This approach has nothing to do with a "let's figure out your core values" retreat routinely administered by snappily-dressed management consultants. Often, these result in hollow efforts focused on nothing more than completing the exercise and putting things down on paper that "look good".

NEWS FLASH: There is no "one-size fits all" core that can be slipped inside any organization. This stuff can't be faked or intellectualized. Instead of fretting about what your brand essence and the values you "should" hold, concentrate on determining with clarity the core principles you "actually" live, believe in, and aspire to. Your brand essence and the things you stand for – and against - are yours alone.

Becoming "seamless" means leveraging the full impact of your brand essence - not only at the 30-foot billboard level - but linking it to the 3-foot level between customer and front-line as well as the 30,000 people who hear your radio commercial or the 300,000,000 who visit your website.

Fundamental shifts in thinking demand new perspectives on how we see the world and the way business works. Despite living and working each day in a world where nothing is fixed, when everything and everyone is continually moving (while listening to an iPod), many of us still crave immobile, rigid structures that satisfy our hunger for fixed solutions; ones that can be neatly placed in the rows of boxes that occupy shelf space in the mind.

Do you realize that thinking about business from the top-down vertical org chart perspective practically guarantees a culture where people become shielded in their armour? Hiding in cubicles, safe within corporate wombs. That was OK back in the sixties, seventies and eighties when there were no open source conversations. Back then, no one in Topeka was blogging, podcasting, texting or e-mailing friends in Toronto or Tokyo. Today, anyone on the planet can find out with a single click, whether your brand makes and keeps its promises. You still control your brand values and identity, but its worth is increasingly determined by conversations you have no control over.

Your challenge has shifted to learning how to lead and manage an organization and brand that, like it or not, comes with an open structure. And you can choose the path your brand will follow either by design or default.

Consciously, or not, companies decide each day whether they are building their brands around hierarchies or relationships. As of this writing, if MySpace were a country, it would rank as the fifth most populated nation in the world. One in three Canadians (nine million-plus) are on Facebook. This onslaught of new media allows any brand to worry less about geography, demographics and marketing to the crowd. Instead, the focus is turning to the creation of tribes and communities able to buy products and services and interact seamlessly - at any number of touch points – on-line or off.

Can you dig in and discover the essence of your brand and a promise worth sharing and spreading? Are you able to peel away stale words, flawed images, and preconceptions until there is nothing left but the core and discover what truly makes your brand remarkable?

This process may involve asking for some outside help. It can be very difficult to "see the picture when you are standing in the frame". Perhaps you will find a trusted friend, or a respected outsider, brave enough to talk plainly, to help you see what your brand is really all about - with uncommon clarity.

But be careful.

The truth might sting a little.

Is your brand ready to flip, flop and surf in our flat, digitized world?

Are you open to basing your brand strategy on a timeless, principle-centered framework, built to withstand future technological change? A model that draws and leverages strength from an intangible, inner core, based on unshakeable beliefs and an uncommonly remarkable promise?

Becoming "seamless" is not easy for any organization. But, in the case of WestJet and the people it touches, it is well worth the effort. For all intents and purposes, "seamless" represents an ideal. Unattainable perfection in the making and delivery of a brand promise. However, chasing perfection may allow your brand to shine as it catches excellence along the way.

Answers to three core questions reveal the essence of "seamless" branding:

1. What promise are you making?
2. In what way is your promise remarkable and relevant?
3. Is your business aligned internally to fulfill that promise?

Most companies are nothing more than a collection of tangible assets such as buildings and equipment; products and services to be sold; replaceable bodies filling boxes on an org chart.

But, any business can be newly calibrated so people have an opportunity to build something bigger than themselves.

And make a difference in ways not even you can imagine.

We shape clay into a pot,
but it is the emptiness inside
that holds whatever we want.

We hammer wood for a house,
but it is the inner space
that makes it livable.

We join spokes together in a wheel,
but it is the centre hole
that makes the wagon move.
-LAO TZU, 145 B.C.

35

Nuts, Bolts And
A Few Loose Screws

"Yes, there are two paths you can go by, but in the long run, there's still time to change the road you're on"
-ROBERT PLANT

L.T. has never been to Kashmir, but she does have two university degrees.

A Bachelor of Science and an MBA.

Cash flow projections, GANT charts, and building operational plans are child's play for L.T. Few can play cerebral hopscotch the way L.T. can; analyzing sales volume, fixed and hidden costs, profit margins and inventory churn to reveal formulaic solutions for business success.

L.T. is a classic linear, logical, left-brained, nuts and bolts thinker, often regarded as the most smarticle person in the boardroom, but still someone with a bustle in her business hedgerow.

"I routinely rejected air-fairy, artsy-fartsy, blue-sky dreamers as unfocused, and without discipline. Grandiose thinkers without any hope of ever achieving anything real. That's why I favoured methodical, strategic, logical, well thought out strategies to get things done in a timely, efficient, productive manner. My mantra for many years has been, 'If you can't measure it, don't bother doing it.' That's why nebulous concepts like 'Pay it Forward' meant nothing to me. There was no way those initiatives could be quantified."

"But, one day I woke up to find myself pretty much the only left-brain thinker in the room, surrounded by creative types, spending hours in meetings that seemed to go nowhere. I used to sit there, look at my watch and wonder 'what's the point'? Rather arrogant of me - when you consider that the organization

I'm part of has achieved more than most small businesses could ever hope to accomplish in a lifetime."

"Then one day, an idea fell on me like a ton of bricks."

What L.T. discovered is the essence of *Nuts, Bolts And A Few Loose Screws*. A metaphorical dichotomy, describing how people who are polar opposites in their thinking styles, mesh for optimal business and team success.

met a phor - A figure of speech in which a word or phrase that ordinarily designates one thing is used to designate another, thus making an implicit comparison. Ex: "All the world's a stage".

di chot o my - A division of two mutually exclusive, opposed, or contradictory groups: a dichotomy between thought and action.

Dichotomies are common.

In "The Argument Culture", Deborah Tannen suggests Western society's cultural dialogue is characterized by a warlike atmosphere in which the winning side attempts to display truth as one would a trophy. Listen to everyday conversations unfolding around you and notice the communication breakdowns triggered by any number of subjects:

- Men vs. Women
- Independence or Intimacy
- Good vs. Evil
- Heaven and Hell
- Practical vs. Theoretical
- Tangible or Intangible
- Medicinal vs. Holistic
- Liberal or Conservative
- Justice vs. Mercy
- Offence and Defence
- Red Sox vs. Yankees
- Intellect and Intuition

Typically, opposing ideas produce either-or arguments, each side trying to prove the other wrong. Conceptually, *Nuts, Bolts & a Few Loose Screws* focuses on the mix of left-brain intellects and right-brain intuitives found in most companies – each believing their way of thinking is the only path you can go by.

Our brains are divided into two hemispheres. The left hemisphere is linear and logical' analytical and sequential. The right hemisphere is a nonlinear, chaotic, holistic house of emotion and intuition. Consequently, in most businesses, left-brain – or "nuts & bolts" thinkers, tend to dwell on areas such as:

- Key Performance Indicators
- Strategic Planning
- Budgets and Forecasting
- Return on Investment
- Income Statements
- Balance Sheets

However, some companies cage different animals altogether. Often regarded as having a "few loose screws", these right-brainers relish chewing on abstract bones such as:

- Compelling Sagas
- Symbols, Rituals & "Tribes"
- Character Diamonds
- Brand Essence
- "Blue Oceans" and "Purple Cows"
- Distinctive Design

Roger Martin, dean of the Rotman School of Management, argues that far too often, business leaders settle for simple tradeoffs. Products can be cheap or reliable, but not both. In his book, "The Opposable Mind" Martin contends the best thinkers are those who can transcend the either/or perspective and find new solutions. In a perfect world, we would all utilize what Martin calls "integrative thinking" to examine problems as a whole, embrace the tension between opposing ideas and create new alternatives.

However, there aren't many integrated thinkers to begin with - and because the left/right brain dichotomy is so pronounced, Nuts, Bolts & a Few Loose Screws offers a practical alternative in recognizing and embracing what the other side brings to the table. In other words, no one - not even you - has all the answers to the challenges your team faces each day. However, your ability to innovate and discover new ideas escalates when a collaborative platform emerges with those who are radically "different" from yourself in the way they view the misty mountain world of business.

This is precisely what happened when a mental levee broke with L.T.

"Usually it's purely by accident that you stumble into a situation where you realize that collaboration with the opposite side actually produces an outcome far greater than either side could do on their own. It's like buried treasure. And if you haven't discovered this 'secret', you could spend your entire career thinking your way is the only way and getting frustrated by the other side".

"A lot of my work depends on being able to deliver training presentations, often with team members more than a little on the screwy side. At first, it felt like I was working with children. They were loud. They played what I thought were silly games. We would constantly run over schedule without covering all the agenda topics. And if you're an organized person like me you tend to want to keep your world that way. I think our natural instinct is to fight to hold on to what we know and I wasn't buying all this free-flowing creativity and improvisation. With each session I was getting more and more pissed off and not enjoying it"

"One day, after a sobering evaluation from some training participants, I had an epiphany of sorts when I asked myself 'What if I could communicate my left-brain principles in a better way. What if I could share some stories and use right-brain analogies, metaphors and music to drive home the points I was trying to make. And what if I stopped being the hero in my own movie and let the participants be the stars?' This is not the type of thinking that comes naturally to a nuts & bolts type thinker. But if you haven't allowed yourself to slurp from the soup of intuition, you are not going to be able to access this. You will get trapped by the need to be accurate, proper, professional, superior and wind up trying to pretend you are smarter than everyone else.

Two years ago, I never would have imagined that I would feel so comfortable in front of an audience that I could adlib, create new content on the spot and dance to the theme song of the Austin Powers movies. Yeah baby yeah"!

L.T.'s presentation skills have been elevated to the point where invitations have started rolling in to address business seminars and international conferences. As a speaker, L.T. delights audiences with a unique combination of hard-core facts and humility, mixing wit with wisdom while generating rave reviews from attendees. Achieving that comfort level, however, proved to be impossible until L.T. was able to let go, mentally float over the hills and far away with the added perspectives of more 'screwy' collaborators.

Unfortunately, most business people do not seek out these types of collaborations. Hardly surprising when you consider the way hierarchical, command-and-control institutions promote self advancement - often at the expense of others. Real or imagined vertical, top-down structures called org charts frequently impede any 'colouring outside the lines' within these Courtrooms of Logic. However, flat, horizontally shaped, team-oriented seamless brands encourage experimentation, exploration and splashing in a pool of collaboration at Waterslide Parks of Imagination.

Nuts, Bolts & a Few Loose Screws collaborations hinge on unusually high levels of trust – which only become possible with a serious investment of humility, time, and a willingness to step into different worlds. Without the anchor of trusting relationships, a "nuts & bolts" Intellectual will find the rants and ramblings of a "loose screw" Intuitive to be annoying, distracting and irrelevant. As you might expect, the opposite is also true. Without feeling the presence of genuine, mutual respect, the "loose screw" will find themselves trampled underfoot by the bone-dry approach of a "nuts and bolts" thinker craving "just the facts".

Intellect is linear.

Intuition is not.

Intuition rarely depends on proof, evidence and statistics. Because of this, the intellect can rarely be convinced of an idea's merits until much later - once all the facts are in. But the greatest leaders, explorers, inventors, artists and entrepreneurs never depended on facts alone to dictate what their intuition told them was the right thing to do. If they had, Ghandi's quest for independence would have been de-railed; Columbus would never have sailed; Edison and Ford would have failed.

And Led Zeppelin would have bailed.

Critics hated them, Top 40 radio ignored them, but Led Zeppelin achieved unparalleled success by embracing opposites comparable to the *Nuts, Bolts And A Few Loose Screws* dichotomy.

"Our music should be a marriage of blues, hard rock and acoustic music topped with heavy choruses" and *"lots of light and shade"*   **-JIMMY PAGE**

With more than 200 million records sold worldwide, Led Zeppelin saw each one of their original studio albums reach the *Billboard* Top Ten, with six hitting the Number One spot. *Rolling Stone* magazine described Led Zeppelin as "the heaviest band of all time" and "the biggest band of the '70s.

On the one hand, Led Zep offered chord-crunching guitar riffs that helped define the entire genre of classic rock. On the other hand, the British quartet drew from many sources, incorporating melodic, acoustic sounds that leveraged folk, blues, reggae, soul, and a number of other genres including Celtic, Arabic, Latin and country. Even the band's name, playing on the concept of a "lead balloon", was chosen to reflect the contrast between "heavy" and "light".

Perhaps the pinnacle of Led Zeppelin's commercial and critical success was achieved when record buyers picked up their untitled fourth album, adorned with a city/country visual dichotomy. According to guitarist Jimmy Page, "Stairway to Heaven" crystallized the essence of the band; a musical milestone that fused symbolic words and concepts within an acoustical/electrical marriage that became one of the most-played songs on rock radio, despite never being released as a single.

Within the group itself, Londoners Page and bassist John Paul Jones were trained, professional studio players, able to read and compose music, while singer Robert Plant and drummer

John Bonham were self-taught minstrels from the Midlands who learned by ear and played on feel. In many respects, Led Zeppelin is but one demonstration of how opposing forces and influences can work in unison towards a greater purpose and result. Whether you are building a band or a business, collaborating on a plan or a project, you bring your strength to it. Typically, we tend to concentrate on using our preferred thinking styles and since there is only so much time and energy, it gets channeled from the place we find more comfortable. It could be left-brain logical or right-brain intuitive, and while it is critical to recognize what you bring to the dance, it's even more important to identify what you need.

A business is bigger than you.

Bring only one side to the decision-making table, and allow that side to dominate without leveraging the other, the business will pay the price.

The business will never become all that it can be. The whole never becomes greater than the sum of its parts. For a band or a business to operate effectively, its control centre needs to function like the two hemispheres of the brain with left-right balance. And move from coexisting or conflicting to complementing and collaborating.

Intellect is as important as it ever has been. Intuition alone won't launch a space shuttle or discover a cure for cancer. Without focus and structure, the intuitive often resembles an octopus on roller skates. But that doesn't make the intellect superior. Relying on left-brain logic alone has left many organizations dazed and confused by unprecedented change, unable to detect underlying chaotic patterns that pinpoint threats and opportunities. F. Scott Fitzgerald once wrote, "a sign of 'first-rate intelligence' is the ability 'to hold two opposing ideas in mind at the same time and still be able to function". And a sure sign of first-rate business intelligence is recognizing two diametrically opposing ideas, weaving them into a new model superior to either.

As a society and as individuals, we accumulate knowledge at an exponential rate - yet if you look around, some companies are becoming dumb and dumber, clinging fiercely to hierarchical structures and traditional mindsets. Ideas and talents are hoarded in organizational silos, covering butts and protecting the status quo. But, the moment a fusion of *Nuts, Bolts & a Few Loose Screws* transpires, a chain reaction of intellectual and intuitive knowledge is released; with tipping point potential to reach to reach stratospheric levels.

Does your company's culture actively encourage you to connect with people who complement what you bring to the table? Have you given any thought to the cost involved when a business fails to release the untapped potential of its people in the way they work together? Can you envision the R.O.I. (Return On Imagination) when your left-brained nuts & bolts types seamlessly rock and roll with their screwy, often misunderstood, right-brained team mates?

A new day is dawning. And if you listen very hard, a distinctively different collaborative tune will come to you at last.

Will the shadows of your business and your brand become taller than your soul?

"I'm quite prepared for the possibility that the next revolution is not going to come from a machine. It's going to come from creating a more thoughtful work force and giving people the opportunity to be thoughtful" **-MALCOLM GLADWELL**

Epilogue
Path to the Promise

"Begin with the end in mind."

Stephen Covey declared it to be Habit #2 in his legendary best-seller, *The 7 Habits of Highly Effective People*. Essentially, Covey was describing how all things are created twice.

First, we imagine them in our minds.

Then we do the heavy lifting required to bring them into physical existence.

Crafting a brand that aspires to become "seamless" becomes clear when you apply this principle through the course of constructing a blueprint based on the framework explained earlier in this book. Just as architects and contractors rely on conceptual drawings to provide a sense of order to the construction process, the same approach can be used to lay a foundation for your Seamless Brand™ before any framing or finishing is applied.

Essentially, these 12 Steps, when followed, can save an inordinate amount of time, marketing dollars and Excedrin-level brand disconnect headaches.

1. Discover and Articulate your Brand Essence.

OBJECTIVE: *To identify and understand the personality and patterns that affect brand design (values, experiences and vision).*

Years ago, a group of business executives touring an automotive plant came across one of the workers, a middle-aged lady assembling seat belt components. "What is it you do here in this factory?" asked one of the suits. The woman wearing overalls looked up and replied "I'm saving lives".

Brand Essence is a way of articulating the emotional connection and lasting impression -- usually captured with a single, simple statement or phrase -- that defines the qualities, personality and uniqueness of a brand. Think of it as the soul of the brand, characterizing what the brand stands for.

Brand Essence should never be confused with taglines that

communicate a strategic position. The function of essence is to communicate and energize those inside the organization while a tag line's function is to communicate with the external audience.

Brand essence tends to be timeless and long term - while tag lines could have a short shelf life or be adapted and altered going forward.

Brand Essence can be clarified this way:

- What is your journey about?
- What do you want to be known for?
- What lies behind the inspiration for your business?

2. Clearly Define the Business Model

OBJECTIVE: *To identify the most significant opportunity for growth and sustainability.*

Are you building a goose that becomes an enduring brand or are you collecting golden eggs of immediate, here-and-now revenue? Both approaches have their pros and cons but these must be clarified in order to formulate a business strategy going forward. Is there a "Hedgehog Concept" you can build your business around, reducing complexity to one simple thing? And will it permit your business model to be duplicated and systemized?

In his landmark work, *Good to Great,* Jim Collins contends that "Good is the enemy of great." The "Hedgehog Concept" is a turning point in that journey. Typically, it requires a willingness to address brutal facts over an extended period of time to arrive at a deep understanding of the "Hedgehog Concept". Collins recommends getting the right people involved asking the right questions; being able to autopsy results without blame; learn from the results and gain clarity from answering the following three questions:

- What drives your economic engine?
- What can you be the best in the world at?
- What are you deeply passionate about?

3. Executive Focus

OBJECTIVE: *To accelerate disciplined thought and action.*

Are you prepared to demonstrate Professional Will? An unwavering focus on doing the right things for the long term good of your brand? Or, are you thinking more about 'Built to Flip' than 'Built to Last'? Do you possess the level of Personal Humility required to selflessly shun the limelight and deflect credit for success to others and avoid de-motivating others?

Executive Focus can be established this way:

- What are the most brutal facts of your current reality?
- How do you avoid de-motivating those around you?
- How will you determine what to work on - and what to ignore?

4. Determine your Brand Promise

OBJECTIVE: *To translate the intangibles into something people can rally around (mission, guiding behaviours and definitive statement).*

A believable brand promise can inspire you to do everything from lure you to a fast food drive-thru to make you want to reach out and hug your used car dealer. However, the lasting strength of any brand is determined by its ability to not only make - but to keep - a promise. Eventually you discover that you don't brand your customers, they brand you.

How they do that will be determined by what your brand is promising and the ability of your organization to keep that promise.

- At its very core, what does your business exist to do?
- Can this be observed in the way you serve customers? Would they agree?
- How do you effectively communicate your purpose?

5. Crafting the Brand "Story"

OBJECTIVE: *To write a compelling saga for your business.*

Customers do not buy products. And people don't follow leaders.

Customers buy stories about who you are and what your brand or leadership style represents. This often entails a trip down memory lane and a dig into your past to discern a "story" that would make people care.

- How did you get here?
- What story can you tell that your team can rally around?
- What are people doing to communicate your story on a consistent basis?

6. Inspire Team Engagement
OBJECTIVE: *To identify the emotional fuel for the creation of a tribal environment.*

Most marketing doesn't happen in the marketing department.

Although about half of all employees say they understand the concept of brand, the idea of "delivering the brand" does not translate easily. Studies show that only 15% of employees typically understand their company's brand and even fewer "bleed it" - despite what senior managers believe. And "marketing", the function responsible for defining and implementing the brand, has little, if anything, to do with managing mission critical employee interactions with customers.

Customers pay attention to all interactions with a company, and quietly (and sometimes not-so-quietly) decide whether the marketing promises being made are being kept through the people delivering the products and services.

- What are your people playing for?
- What symbols provide a sense of connectedness?
- What rituals support a larger team purpose?

7. Talent Acquisition Strategy
OBJECTIVE: *To know who should be on your bus and why.*
What is the purpose of an organization?

If the purpose of a business can be defined as creating and keeping customers, the purpose of an organization is to enable otherwise common people to do uncommon things.

The selection of those people represents the best control an organization has on how things get done. People decisions dictate the performance capacity of any brand and as such, who gets recruited, hired, placed or promoted will largely determine how the growth of your brand.

- What is the most critical building block for brand-fit?
- How will brand culture be integrated into your hiring process?
- What specific benchmarks will serve to evaluate position requirements?

8. Creating Customers

OBJECTIVE: *To build a relationship-first strategy.*

How well do you understand your competitive environment? Just what is the size of your pond and how many fish share it with you?

But wait ... there is more!

Is your selling process based on a 'push' or a 'pull' philosophy? How much thought have you given to "dating potential prospects before they "marry" your brand? What gravitational forces exist that would attract prospects to your brand and how easy is it for them to buy from you?

- Who is your primary customer type?
- What language does your customer speak?
- How will you create an effective attraction-formula?

9. Keeping Customers

OBJECTIVE: *To identify current touch-points and areas for improvement.*

How you answer the phone. How they are greeted when they walk through your door or visit your website. Each "touch point" is an interaction with a potential or current customer that will either enhance or diminish brand strength.

Each interaction is a valuable opportunity to win over a new customer or solidify a current relationship. This is what helps build word of mouth buzz.

- What type of customer experience are you trying to create?
- What are your on-site 'WOW' factors for customers?
- What 'WOW' factors will you deliver once they leave?

10. Visual Branding

OBJECTIVE: *To assess the significance of how you are noticed and perceived.*

Long before the days of the "Wild West", Egyptians were branding their cattle in order to identify them 3000 years BC. But what was once used to visually signify ownership has now evolved into a mark of distinction.

Your visual brand either stand outs or blends in with the rest of the herd.

- Is your brand's essence accurately reflected by what people see?
- Are you consistent in the application of your visual touch-points?
- Are the fundamentals of your visual identity solid?

11. Brand Message

OBJECTIVE: *To clarify and sharpen external message.*

Have you chosen powerful words that accurately reflect and powerfully illuminate your brand promise? Do have a clear message that effectively slices through the "white noise" pollution and is easily heard over the herd?

How often you say something - and who you say it to - matters far less than what you say. Repetition and reaching the "right people" pales in comparison to having a message that impresses those who hear it.

- What are you currently known for in your market?
- How relevant and distinctive is your message?
- What can you do to amplify your message?

12. Marketing Strategy

OBJECTIVE: *To evaluate current marketing tactics and adjust if need be.*

Have you determined the best vehicles to deliver your message? Do you know where your primary customers tend to gather and flock together?

Like the tribes of centuries past, today's consumers link to one another by common interests and ideas. Would you prefer marketing to "the crowd" or do you see a way to create a tribe (like Mac addicts) connected by shared beliefs?

- What are you doing to anchor your message in your customers' mind?
- How are you determining your marketing budget?
- What can you do differently to leverage the value of your current assets?

Brands that aspire to becoming "seamless" need to have at least some idea of where the highway is headed. Call it a blueprint, roadmap or what you will, but be conscious of one thing - no one intends to a climb ladder leaning against the wrong wall. Unfortunately, that's what often happens when a lack of clarity - and little if any planning - prevents a business or personal brand from achieving its true potential.

In *The 7 Habits*, Stephen Covey asks you to imagine that, when all is said and done and you're about to ascend into heaven, what if you could listen in to what was being said at your funeral?

Imagine applying the same "end in mind" visualization exercise for your brand.

How "seamless" could it become?

"Everybody wants to go to heaven, but nobody wants to die to get there."

-PETER TOSH

About the Author

Gair Maxwell has been called unconventional at times. Thank you, it's true.

His international debut as a published author resulted from a 4 a.m. visit to a local coffee shop, simply through his willingness to accept a challenge to just watch, listen and learn.

And then do something about it.

He is co-founder and a driving force behind The Seamless Brand. More and more companies are turning to **The Seamless Brand Program™** and its unique process to seamlessly align external marketing to internal culture or as Gair explains "to make and more importantly, keep a promise that matters".

A former radio & television host, he racked up more than 10,000 interviews and 30,000 broadcasts in a two-decade career that included stints in his hometown of Moncton NB as well as Calgary and Red Deer, Alberta where he worked alongside future Hockey Night in Canada host Ron MacLean.

As a professional speaker, Gair delivers close to 100 presentations a year. He is a member of the Canadian Association of Professional Speakers, NSA, IFFPS, and is the author of "The Seamless Brand" blog, which entertains and inspires readers in more than 70 countries each business day. He is also a contributing author through Wizard Academy Press in Austin, TX to "People Stories – Inside the Outside, released in April of 2006.

A busy father of two grown children and a grandfather to Cayden, Gair plays golf in the 90's, rocks to music of the 80's and became a lifelong fan of the Pittsburgh Steelers back in the 70's. Active in his community as a volunteer on many causes and projects, he also completed his first marathon in 2005 with less than a week of preparation.

Like we said ... a little unconventional.

He resides in the most honest city in North America, Moncton, NB Canada.

Seamless Factoids...

The Gallup organization polled 6,000 passengers and discovered that by a ratio of 3-4 to 1 employees are more important than advertising messages in building brand loyalty.

MORI Research (UK)

Over 80% of companies believe they have fantastic customer experiences. Only 8% of their customers agree.

HARVARD CASE STUDY

61% of customers don't believe technology has improved customer service

ACCENTURE SURVEY

40% of marketing investment is wasted as mis-informed or demotivated staff behaviour unwittingly undermines the promotional promise. 68% of customers eventually leave because of the indifferent way in which they were treated.

DARREN SEARS, The Seamless Brand

Companies could boost profitability by 25-100% by increasing their customer retention rate by just 5%.

FREDERICK REICHHELD, Author, "The Loyalty Effect"

44% of Americans do not believe anything that comes out of the mouths of companies.

HARRIS POLL, 2007

Gratitude's

Dr. Deepak Chopra explains in the "7 Spiritual Laws of Success" that achieving success is governed by the same laws that govern all of nature; which is to judge nothing and be grateful for everything. As Chopra puts it, "Think of all the things you're grateful for. If you just do that, you can't have ego and gratitude at the same time". Psychologist Alice Isen of Cornell University adds, expressing gratitude triggers a release of dopamine, the chemical in the brain associated with happiness. "It activates the parts of the brain in which complex thinking and conflict resolution are thought to be headquartered."

It is with a grateful heart and a dopamine-filled head, the author sincerely thanks the people who helped bring *"Nuts, Bolts And a Few Loose Screws"* to the publishing finish line.

Mucho appreciation goes to favorite son Ryan Maxwell and hard-working Sean Taylor of Wizard Academy Press for their invaluable visual and editorial input. The dynamic Dana Zilic literally parachuted in from heaven, supplying a most alchemic mixture of 11th-hour manuscript critiques while the cerebral Katherine Grant performed yeoman duty through some laborious proof-reading.

As you might expect, a project of this nature had many friends, benefactors and influencers along the way. In random order, they include:

Allan Power, Ken LeBlanc, Dale Betts, Jeremy Demont, Walter Melanson, Jim & Dawna Gilbert, Dave MacKenzie, Darren Sears, Silvy Moleman, Ian Varty, Daniel Gillis, Sandy Gillis, Jerry Simmons,

Ronnie LeBlanc, The Four Divas (Sharon Geldart, Debbie Brine, Mary O'Donnell, Valerie Roy), Tyson Matheson, Leanne Taylor, Danielle Leger, Lisa Stutt, Bill Bishop, Don Schmincke, Mandy McLean, Botsford Productions, everyone at The Seamless Brand and the thousands that have attended more than a decade of seminars and workshops that provided countless insights that helped shape some of these ideas along the way.

Extra special thanks to Doug Stevenson for introducing "Story Theatre Method" and sharing it with the world.

Supremo extra special thanks to Roy H. Williams, who impacts thousands of lives every day from an idyllic 30-acre campus about 20 minutes of Austin, TX. This book owes its existence to the vision of Roy and "Princess Pennie" when they opened up their hearts and the magical world that is Wizard Academy.

"Of all the 'attitudes' we can acquire, surely the attitude of gratitude is the most important and by far the most life-changing"

-ZIG ZIGLAR

What is Wizard Academy?

Composed of a fascinating series of workshops led by some of the most accomplished instructors in America, Wizard Academy is a progressive new kind of business and communications school whose stated objective is to improve the creative thinking and communication skills of sales professionals, internet professionals, business owners, educators, ad writers, ministers, authors, inventors, journalists and CEOs.

Founded in 1999, the Academy has exploded into a worldwide phenomenon with an impressive fraternity of alumni who are rapidly forming an important worldwide network of business relationships.

"Alice in Wonderland on steroids! I wish Roy Williams had been my very first college professor. If he had been, everything I learned after that would have made a lot more sense and been a lot more useful... Astounding stuff."

—Dr. Larry McCleary,
Neurologist and Theoretical Physicist

"...Valuable, helpful, insightful, and thought provoking. We're recommending it to everyone we see."

—Jan Nations and Sterling Tarrant
senior managers, Focus on the Family

"Be prepared to take a wild, three-ring-circus journey into the creative recesses of the brain...[that] will change your approach to managing and marketing your business forever. For anyone who must think critically or write creatively on the job, the Wizard Academy is a must."

—Dr. Kevin Ryan
Pres., The Executive Writer

"Even with all I knew, I was not fully prepared for the experience I had at the Academy... Who else but a wizard can make sense of so many divergent ideas? I highly recommend it."

—Mark Huffman,
Advertising Production Manager, Procter & Gamble

"A life-altering 72 hours."

—Jim Rubart

**To learn more about Wizard Academy,
visit www.WizardAcademy.org or
call the academy at (800) 425-4769**